Tranquillity and Ruin

Also by Danyl McLauchlan

Unspeakable Secrets of the Aro Valley (2013)

Mysterious Mysteries of the Aro Valley (2016)

Tranquillity and Ruin

Danyl McLauchlan

Victoria University of Wellington Press

Victoria University of Wellington Press
PO Box 600 Wellington
New Zealand
vup.wgtn.ac.nz

A catalogue record is available from the
National Library of New Zealand.

ISBN 9781776564118

Printed in Singapore by Markono Print Media Pte Ltd

for Maggie and Sadie

Contents

Foreword

The book is about tranquillity and ruin. But when I was writing it, I told people it was about uncertainty. Which was technically true. I didn't know what these essays had in common, in terms of a grand theme: they were just separate, mostly unrelated subjects I was obsessed with. 'Uncertainty' sounded important and cerebral while being vague enough to mean anything. But now that they're finished, I wonder if I was onto something there.

I wrote this book in a state of uncertainty about subjects I used to hold very strong views on. In my twenties I worked in the tech industry, then I studied genetics and wound up on the technical team of my university's biology department. I published two novels and wrote reviews and political columns. I helped out progressive politicians and worked on an election campaign. And all of this was accompanied by high degrees of certainty about the value of science and technology and progressive politics and rationalism and literature. I haven't abandoned my beliefs about any of these things, exactly. I'm just a lot less certain about them than I used to be.

The first two essays are about mood disorders and meditation, and about uncertainty as statisticians and psychologists use the term. Some people with depression and/or anxiety suffer terribly, but I was pretty lucky: diagnosed quickly, I responded well to medication, tapered off it again without too much misery. But I'd always thought of myself as a stable, *very* rational person, so living through periods in which I was not especially sane required some adjustment to my self-image.

Having a mood disorder is a bit like having a bad back. It never quite goes away and you have to manage the condition because if you don't it flares up and ruins everything at exactly the worst time. After some trial and error I found that meditating for half an hour every morning and evening was the best way to not get depressed. This was good for my mental health but terrible for my identity as an arch-rational sceptic. Meditation seemed so mystical and new-agey and none of the mostly terrible books I read on the subject could explain to me why it worked. I'm not a psychologist, or remotely qualified to give mental health advice, but I offer up these essays to anyone who is mindfulness-curious yet repulsed by the mists of gibberish that obscure the subject. They're an attempt to build a palatable-to-sceptics framework around meditation and the odd and intriguing things that happen to you when you meditate a lot.

The third essay was written in a state of political uncertainty. In June of 2018 I went to a protest outside the US Embassy in Wellington. It was early evening, midwinter, extremely cold. The protest was an anti-Trump event. Earlier that week the US media had reported on the Trump administration's family separation policy, in which the children of illegal migrants entering the US from Mexico were taken from their parents and placed in custody. Young children were being confined alone, in terrible conditions. I wanted to do something and going along to a protest was something, so I did that.

A large crowd turned out for the event, but the embassy was deserted. It was undergoing refurbishment: the buildings were concrete shells adjacent to mounds of dug-up earth, all lit orange by the mounted security lights. We were protesting a construction site rather than a diplomatic post. But I ran into a friend in the crowd who was a PR advisor for a government department. 'It doesn't matter if there's no one in the buildings,' she assured me. 'What matters is the symbolism and extent of the media coverage.' We looked around to see where the news crews were setting up, but there weren't any.

'We don't trust the mainstream media,' one of the organisers explained to us. 'But you can share it on your social media channels.' So we all stood in the darkness in front of a hollowed-out building, our breath misting, while different activists took turns standing on the wall beside the gates denouncing neoliberalism and Trump, and people in the crowd took selfies.

I left early, frustrated by the pointlessness of it all. Walking home it occurred to me that I'd felt this way before, many times over my decades lurking on the periphery of protests and progressive political and activist groups. It was never clear to me whether anyone was doing anything useful or just pretending to do stuff to feel better about ourselves.

The political scientist Eitan Hersh calls this 'political hobbyism'. This is when you think of yourself as a committed, political person. You consume vast amounts of books and media and have really sophisticated and informed views about a range of issues. You go online and advocate for those views, or critique or mock people with different ones. You're happy when elections or other political outcomes go your way and devastated when they don't. And you feel worthy and smart. But, Hersh argues, none of this media consumption or online activism does anything. None of it helps anyone. It's purely about the emotional and intellectual needs of the activist, who is usually educated and financially comfortable and enjoying the fantasy that they're changing the world, without actually changing anything. It's like being a sports fan but with an unearned sense of moral worth built into the fandom.

This is a painfully accurate description of most of my political activity for maybe ten to fifteen years. I did do some worthwhile work for a political party, but electoral and party politics is stressful and adversarial. It's an environment some people flourish in, but I wasn't one of them. And even if you are one of those people, it's hard to change things through democratic politics. Most political contests are zero-sum: no matter what you're doing there's a group of smart, hard-working people in another party or faction trying to stop you, and the people fighting for the status quo usually win. Even if you somehow gain power, government in developed democracies is deeply constrained: political leaders are bounded on all sides by path dependency, elite consensus, market and public sector limitations and the narrow window of public opinion. I don't want to sound too cynical or contrarian about politics. Some problems can only be solved politically; some politicians do enormous good. Some of my best friends really are politicians.

But by the time I wrote this essay, I'd begun to suspect that an increasing amount of political activism manifests as hobbyism, and changes nothing, and even if it isn't, it runs into the zero-sum problem of the adversarial system and also changes nothing. Which is why I was so intrigued by the effective altruists, who mostly see government and electoral politics as barriers to change. To them, politics is something you route around. Change is something that requires both sacrifice and intellectual humility. It requires uncertainty, in other words, about the efficacy of what you're trying to do and why you're doing it.

The effective altruists make some people uncomfortable. A few early readers of this essay wanted me to explain why they were wrong about everything. The very nature of effective altruism means that the effective altruists also worry about whether they're wrong, and one of the few things I am now more certain of is that this uncertainty and self-doubt is an important component of real change.

The last essay is set in a Buddhist monastery not far from my home. I didn't go there to write about it. I just wanted a place to meditate that was more convenient than the beautiful but extremely remote retreat I visited in the second essay.

Bodhinyanarama is on the edge of a large commuter suburb. People walk their dogs through the grounds in the evening. The monks beg for alms at the local shops. The overlap highlights the radical difference between the monastic life and the secular world. It reminds us that the way we live now is not the only way to live. We have options.

Our society is very critical of itself. Sometimes its self-loathing feels so intense it's frightening. I feel it too, but while I'm always outraged about the consumerism, the environmental collapse, the inequality, the grand wrongness of it all, I don't ever seem to change anything about my life in response to any of these outrages, and neither does anyone else I know. We all just live our comfortable lives while being censorious of everyone else who lives the same way. But the monks at Bodhinyanarama looked at contemporary society and decided,

'We're not going to live like that.' And they don't.

A monastic life devoted to spiritual values, cemented with vows of poverty and chastity is not for everyone, and it is not for me. But both times I've stayed at the monastery I've thought about how many unhappy people I know, or have known, some of whom literally died of unhappiness, who would have preferred the quiet, communal, non-materialistic, structured society of monastic life. I also know that none of them would have considered it, because a monastic life is a religious life and they are, or were, educated, enlightened atheists. So the final essay tries to find a way for sceptics to be more sympathetic towards religious communities and spiritual value systems.

None of these subjects are original, but most of the books I've read about them were written in a state of maximal certainty, either by fierce critics or true believers. It's hard to find books about meditation or activism or politics or rationalism that are ambivalent about their subject matter. The monks and neuroscientists and philosophers and activists in these essays probably aren't right about everything, but if they're right about a handful of things that the rest of us are wrong about, and if those ideas influence us to change our lives in meaningful ways, then I think they're more valuable than ideas we enthusiastically agree with but which don't inspire us to change anything.

*

I wrote these essays in 2018 and 2019, and I'm writing this foreword during the coronavirus outbreak of early 2020. I'm locked down in my house, with my family, clicking refresh on all the cleverly coded data-visualisation tools that graph the global death toll. I'm reading torrents of news reports and scientific publications and feeling the distinct blend of hyper-informed hysteria and trance-like inertia that, sometime over the last decade, has become the default emotional tone of the twenty-first century.

And I've spent a lot of time thinking about a William Gibson book, *The Peripheral*, a partly post-apocalyptic novel published in 2014. The apocalypse in Gibson's book isn't a nuclear war, or a killer plague. No one turns into a zombie. Technological civilisation does not collapse. Instead, a series of pandemics and climate catastrophes lead to political and economic instability, and over the course of the twenty-first century the population of the planet declines by about 80 per cent. The society on the other side of the apocalypse is neither utopian or dystopian: just a worse version of our current world.

Right now this feels like an awfully persuasive vision of the future. Nothing bad needs to happen to get there: we all just keep doing what we're doing. My book doesn't know how to fix this. I've tried to write about ideas and thinkers who I think are important and relevant to these times, but are unknown, inaccessible or unpalatable for various reasons, and I've tried to make them more comprehensible to a wider audience. Maybe that's something.

I've meditated a lot during the past month, in lockdown, and lately I've started to hear what Buddhist texts call the Nada Sound, also known as the transcendental sound, a mysterious noise meditators often hear in deep meditative states. It is either the cosmic vibration of the universe or the background noise of your auditory cortex, depending on who you ask. For most meditators it is a pleasant sound, like the rustling of leaves or the murmuring of the tide. For me it is like tinnitus—a discordant, atonal drone rising and falling in pitch. And this morning I rose early, sat in my spare room, wrapped myself in a blanket and entered a long, deep, enormously calming meditative state that ended when a bunch of books from the bookshelf behind me fell on my head for no reason at all.

Arise and Pass Away

For weeks I'd been waking in the middle of the night. Sometimes I lay in bed thinking about work. Other nights I had fragments of songs looping in my head. I'd read somewhere that our brains recycle thoughts or pieces of music because it saves energy, and one night I lay awake thinking 'I'm thinking this thought to save energy' over and over again.

And one night I pulled on some trackpants and a sweater and went for a walk. It was about 3am. Very calm. The sky glowed with stars. I could hear the hum of the power lines and the sound of the stream at the bottom of the hill. I could also hear music. A choir. I couldn't make out the tune. Possibly a hymn? My first thought was: someone is playing their stereo way too loud. But then the music stopped, and I heard a man's voice and a woman's laughter and the song began again from the beginning, a little faster and stronger, and I realised the music came from an actual choir of people somewhere nearby.

What kind of choir practised at three in the morning? It sounded as if it came from the school. I crossed the road, treading carefully in my bare feet, and walked up the school driveway. Whoever they were, I thought, it would be nice to stand at the back of the hall and listen to a big group of people singing together. It might calm me down and help me sleep. But when I got to the top of the driveway all the buildings were dark. There was no one there.

There was wind in the trees, and I had to wait for it to die down to get a fix on the sound. Then the singing returned, very clearly: a strong, joyous chant. It came from further down the valley. Which made sense: there was a church over there. The hills must have complicated the acoustics. I set off in that direction, breaking into a light jog.

'An auditory hallucination,' my doctor said the next morning. 'Probably tied to the sleep deprivation.'

'Probably tied? You think?' I slouched in a chair, still dressed in the same trackpants I'd worn the night before, although they were now splattered with mud. I'd tried to follow the music through the unlit tracks of the town green belt at the bottom of the valley before I figured out that it wasn't real and returned home. I'd been awake ever since.

I squinted at my doctor. His office looked out over the harbour. It was a bright autumn day and the light from the sea and clouds turned the windows into blinding squares of silver and white light. The doctor was a vague, shimmering figure in the foreground. All I wanted was to lie down in a dark room and close my eyes.

'Why can't I sleep?' I demanded. 'Why is this happening? I don't drink. I don't take drugs. I've cut out caffeine. I drink peppermint tea now, like an animal. And yet'—I gestured at my mud-stained clothes. 'I can't be wandering around my neighbourhood in the middle of the night, hallucinating. It's completely inappropriate.'

'You say the insomnia started about a month ago,' he said, looking from his notes to a calendar on his computer. 'Which takes us back to daylight saving. Maybe that was the trigger? Sometimes the sleep cycles get confused. We'll try you on sleeping pills for a couple of days, then you can try and sleep without them and see how you go.'

'What if that doesn't work?' I knew there was a link between insomnia and depression, that the conditions amplified each other; I worried that if I didn't treat the insomnia I'd get depressed again, or maybe I was already depressed and that was causing the insomnia. I'd been on antidepressants before. They made me gain weight, made me feel sedated, and coming off them was tedious and difficult. I'd go on them if I had to but I'd really rather not. I explained all this to the doctor in a long, rambling speech. He listened, shimmering patiently, then said, 'From what I'm hearing I think you're suffering from anxiety, not depression.'

'Great. Anxiety. Brilliant.'

'But the medications are the same.'

'Oh.'

The sleeping pills gave me six hours of deep, dreamless sleep at night and a metallic taste in my mouth during the day. After three days I went back to unmedicated sleep and woke in the middle of the night. Same thing the next night. The following morning I went to the pharmacy and filled my prescription for nortriptyline, a tricyclic antidepressant with a side effect of sedation. The box came with bright yellow stickers advising me not to operate heavy machinery or expose myself to bright sunlight.

*

I had a happy childhood followed by a happy life until, in my late thirties and early forties, I went through a series of depressive episodes, panic attacks, insomnia, none of it with any apparent cause. On a scale of suffering it was comparable to having a repeating series of bad colds. (People are not often sympathetic when I tell them this, but bad colds are actually quite bad.) I responded well to the drugs but it seemed absurd that I was taking sleeping pills and antidepressants for a mental illness with no obvious cause, so I discontinued them. I did fine without them for a year or so, and then not so fine and went back on them for a year, and repeated this cycle for about five years. By the time of the hallucinated choir incident I'd been off for about eighteen months and was convinced I'd finally shaken off whatever the hell was wrong with me. So this was a setback. But, I decided, a temporary one. I immediately started plotting to discontinue the new drugs. 'You should try meditating,' my wife Maggie suggested. 'That's supposed to be good for anxiety.'

She'd read this on Facebook, but it turned out to be true. There were plenty of clinical studies out there showing that mindfulness-based therapies had large, robust effect sizes in the treatment of mood disorders. But none of the studies explained what mindfulness was, other than that it was connected to meditation, somehow.

I was sceptical, but it was worth a try. After a couple of months on the nortriptyline I went along to a Buddhist meditation evening. It was held in a church, but the noticeboard was filled with flyers advertising meditation classes, yoga evenings and Tai Chi sessions. The evening was not a success. At least not for me. A monk appeared, shaved head, saffron robes and all, and talked to us about joy and compassion. He told us that mindfulness was 'being in the moment', which meant nothing to me. Weren't we always in the moment? Then we meditated. I sat in my chair in the warm room and tried to focus on the joy in my own life, and to feel compassion towards my fellow conscious beings, but I lost interest in both these subjects after a few seconds. My mind wandered to other things. I felt bored. I spent most of the session thinking about how weird it was to sit in silence with my eyes shut in a room full of strangers. I went home feeling unenlightened and unimpressed.

But I kept researching, in an occasional way, over the next few months. I learned that most popular books on meditation and mindfulness were in the *Quantum Healing*, deep cleanse your aura, learn astral travel for health and profit tradition. But I liked the texts I found on secular Buddhism, a new, loosely organised, very western interpretation of Buddhism, popular with some cognitive psychologists and neuroscientists. Scrolling through an online secular Buddhist discussion forum, I finally found a coherent description of mindfulness.

In 2010, *Science* published a Harvard study in which the authors recruited 2250 research subjects and installed an app on their phones. The app contacted the subjects at random intervals and asked them what they were doing, what they were thinking about, and whether the subject of their thoughts was pleasant, unpleasant or neutral. The finding was that the subjects spent an average of 47 per cent of their waking lives thinking about something other than the task they were doing, 'contemplating events that happened in the past, might happen in the future, or may never happen at all'. And they found that spending more time in this distracted state made the subjects unhappy.

There's a famous William James quote: 'When we reach the end of our days, our life experience will equal what we have paid attention to.' We seem to be happier if we pay attention to the world around us, rather than our own internal thoughts. Daydreaming and fantasising feels nice in the moment but comes at an emotional and cognitive cost. In this framework, mindfulness—stripped of all the mysticism and pretence—is simply the practice of training the mind to pay attention to the world instead of the discursive thoughts, daydreams, plots, fantasies and catastrophising it prefers to indulge in.

Secular Buddhism is very online, and presents itself as philosophical rather than religious—mostly rational, whatever 'rational' means when you're sitting with your eyes closed watching your thoughts dissolve. It's loosely organised around a few texts written by westerners, with titles like *Buddhism Without Beliefs*, *Mastering the Core Teachings of the Buddha*, *The Science of Meditation*, *The Mind Illuminated* (arguably the most popular secular Buddhist text, often abbreviated as TMI: it's exhaustingly long and comprehensive). Secular Buddhists tend to be younger, millennial; science and tech backgrounds are common. The movement reaches a weird apotheosis in Silicon Valley, where meditation is seen as 'hacking the central nervous system', and HR departments mandate corporate mindfulness sessions to optimise productivity. Many of the secular Buddhists I've talked to arrived at meditation through seeking long-term solutions to their mood disorders.

It's hard to point to any central doctrines of the new movement, other than being secular and following the Buddha's path: 'the dharma'. But there's a broad consensus that this is primarily a philosophical and meditative practice rather than a religious faith, that people living in the modern world have access to seclusion and free time that the pre-moderns did not, and this gives us the freedom to meditate without moving to a monastery and becoming a monk or a nun. But, secular Buddhist teachers caution, the same culture that grants us this freedom tries to take it away by presenting us with an infinite number of pleasures and distractions. We can escape this trap, the argument goes, by interpreting the Buddhist texts through a modern lens—drawing from the two and a half thousand years of Buddhist literature and stripping out all the pre-modern cultural and religious baggage. I bought a few of these books, warily, and found the opening chapters to be clear and refreshingly free of religious dogma.

I started meditating every day, half an hour every morning, another half an hour in the evening. The cover illustrations of meditation books often show people's heads exploding with light, but the reality of the practice is that it's mostly just boring and frustrating. One of the most common techniques is simply to sit and pay attention to the sensations of the breath at the nose. When I first started doing this my mind drifted off to other things, then I realised I was distracted so I refocused, and then it drifted again; I brought it back again. And that was it, every day.

The texts were filled with tips on how to overcome mind-wandering. But none of them seemed to work for me. I kept trying, but no matter what I did, discursive thoughts kept breaking through, hurling themselves against my attempts to concentrate like angry drunks in a holding cell. Meditation was hard. It felt pointless. I wanted to give it up. But, somewhat frustratingly, it also worked, in the sense that doing it every day made me much calmer and happier.

'So this is what it's like to be sane,' I marvelled to Maggie. We were grocery shopping. I'd been meditating for about a month, and I felt more focused, less anxious. I beamed at the products in the pets aisle—the automated feeders, the plastic dog bones, the worming tablets—which all glowed with a soft inner light.

'That's great,' she said, genuinely happy for me but also, by now, a little tired of the subject. Then she asked, 'How does it work?'

'It just calms me down. Helps me focus on what's real. Our modern western culture is so distracting and superficial, y'know?'

'Uh huh. But why does it have that effect? What's the mechanism?'

'I'm not sure.' I answered slowly, because that was a really good question.

'You've got that big pile of books,' Maggie said. 'What do they say?'

I wasn't sure. These were lengthy books, and I was a busy guy so I'd skipped over anything that didn't seem immediately relevant to my day-to-day practice. I started to read them again, but they didn't say anything about mood disorders. And, while these authors called themselves secular, the theory and philosophical content were still suspiciously religion-adjacent, I decided. Most of these secular Buddhists were still selling a belief system that seemed not-very-secular, if not downright mystical the more you learned about it. I put the books away again.

But I kept following the practical instructions. Eventually I overcame mind-wandering. I was able to focus on the sensations of my breath instead of drifting off into schemes and fantasies. But the next problem was drowsiness. When the mind is still and quiet, the body assumes it wants to go to sleep. You start to experience dreamlike thoughts and see hypnagogic patterns in the blackness of your eyelids and eventually drift off. This is the stage of the famous 'zen lurch', when you sit down to meditate and focus on the breath but startle awake twenty minutes later, pitching forwards mid-snore.

There are more exercises to overcome drowsiness, and more obstacles beyond it. Next is physical discomfort: your knees hurt, your nose itches. You're supposed to ignore these sensations, which seems impossible until somehow you do. After that you must contend with 'subtle dullness': the awake but still not alert condition in which we spend most of our lives, and there are exercises to increase the power of conscious awareness so that you can see your own thoughts and sensations with sharp clarity. 'The mind becomes like a brightly lit room,' to paraphrase *The Mind Illuminated*. It's a little like weightlifting, or spin class, except for your attention: you get a little stronger each day.

The goal is to be hyperalert but completely calm and focused, resting effortlessly on the sensations of the breath. This is a state of mind that the Buddhists call 'access concentration'. Attention rests on the concentration object and there are no distractions, only faint and barely perceptible wisps of cognition arising in the periphery of your thought then drifting away like dust in beams of sunlight. There is no boredom or sense of time passing because boredom and time are thoughts.

This is an extremely pleasant state of mind. It's comparable to being on powerful painkillers but without the dreamy fuzziness. I found that if I reached it and sat in access concentration for just a few minutes—it is an unstable state, easy to tip out of—I carried a deep sense of focus and calm with me for most of the day. I still felt stress and disappointment and frustration and rage, but the situations that provoked these responses seemed to have the volume turned down, and my mind didn't cultivate self-loathing or rage-inducing thoughts the way it used to.

I discontinued my anxiety medication. Discontinuing was normally a fraught process of mood swings, brain zaps and sleep disruption, but this time it went smoothly: like walking down a gentle grassy incline instead of scrabbling down a steep scree slope. Life reached a new equilibrium. Yes, meditation was time-consuming and boring. Yes, when life got hectic and I stopped meditating because I simply didn't have the time for it, I started waking in the middle of the night again and my anxiety and depression flooded back in. But so long as I kept doing it, the meditation worked. I wasn't sure why, but really, who cared? People talked a lot of nonsense about meditation and mindfulness, I decided. It was just a form of mental exercise. It made you psychologically fitter. That was all.

The French neuroscientist Stanislas Dehaene once wrote about what we'd see if we could look through our eyes directly, without all the mind's real time image processing:

> We never see the world as our retina sees it. In fact, it would be a pretty horrible sight: a highly distorted set of light and dark pixels, blown up toward the center of the retina, masked by blood vessels, with a massive hole at the location of the 'blind spot' where cables leave for the brain; the image would constantly blur and change as our gaze moved around. What we see, instead, is a three-dimensional scene, corrected for retinal defects, mended at the blind spot, stabilized for our eye and head movements, and massively reinterpreted based on our previous experience of similar visual scenes. All these operations unfold unconsciously—although many of them are so complicated that they resist computer-modeling. For instance, our visual system detects the presence of shadows in the image and removes them. At a glance, our brain unconsciously infers the sources of lights and deduces the shape, opacity, reflectance, and luminance of the objects.

I thought about this passage when, about three months into my meditation practice, I had an odd, unsettling experience. I discovered that if I concentrated on the sensations of the breath at my nose for long enough—about forty minutes, which seems to be the magic point for many people—the feeling of continuous conscious sensation, the feeling you'll get right now if you focus on your own breathing, decohered and broke down into a series of discrete, meaningless vibrations. It was a little like saying the same word over and over until it loses its meaning.

It's one thing to know, in theory, that thinking consists of electrochemical constructs in the brain, that we're never really seeing or experiencing the world directly, only a constructed representation of it—but the experience of this was surprisingly upsetting. I kept remembering Yeats's phrase that he was a soul fastened to the body of a dying animal, and I began to regard my body with a certain dread, viewing it as a robot made of meat, a machine designed to transport my brain around and supply it with data and energy. Which of course it is, but I felt that wasn't a healthy way to think about myself.

That summer, while I was on holiday, I increased my meditation practice to an hour a day. I felt elated for hours after each session. But the odd experiences and morbid thoughts intensified. Then, towards the end of one of these hour-long sits, I felt violent jolts of energy in my hands. Two mornings in a row my field of vision went blotchy, then white, then resolved into what I can only call visions. The first was of a gravel embankment leading down to a stream, with a group of men walking up to the road alongside it, their backs to me, tall green trees in the distance. The second was of a Māori family in the late nineteenth century, awkwardly posing for a family photograph on a beach. Neither of these scenes meant anything to me, but both were astonishingly vivid, like seeing something in the world instead of something in my mind. Other times—also when I was deep in the meditative state—I had the sense that something was looking back at me from across a vast distance. I still felt happy, but I worried that my depression and anxiety were manifesting in some new and subtle way, conspiring to make me sick again.

I went back to my books and read them properly, all the way through this time. The reason none of these books talked about mood disorders, I learned, is that the Buddhists don't see meditation as a form of therapy. The point of the practice is not to help unhappy middle-aged men feel content as they drift around the supermarket. Meditation, for the Buddhists, is a tool for uncovering radical hidden truths about the nature of mind and reality. My visions, bizarre sensations and intimations of death weren't manifestations of my mood disorder that the meditation was failing to address. They were caused by the meditation. I was interfering with my central nervous system in ways that weren't covered by the owner's manual.

And these experiences were, from the Buddhist perspective, desirable. They meant that I was getting closer to the hidden truth of things. The goal of the practice is to train the mind to realise the three characteristics that the Buddhists claim are central to existence: the impermanence of the material world, the centrality of suffering and the non-existence of the self. There's no point in understanding any of these things intellectually, the Buddha claimed. You have to meditate and experience them directly, and these experiences can be transformational and, eventually, he claimed, release you from unhappiness. But they can also be troubling—the final appendix in *The Mind Illuminated* is ominously titled 'The Dark Night of the Soul'. The peace and equanimity you gain from mindfulness meditation is designed to help you cope with the insight that you don't really exist, and that everything else you know about reality is allegedly wrong. I'm not a sometimes sleepless, sometimes anxious, sometimes medicated, sometimes depressed, often bewildered middle-aged man, the tradition teaches. I'm not even a person at all, but rather a cacophony of neural algorithms, a flood of impressions and vibrations no more individual and enduring than a fire started at night that burns until daybreak.

*

I felt, and still feel, a little suckered by mindfulness; a little cursed. Meditation is like something I bought off a sinister old man in an antique shop. I always knew, in an absent, abstract way, that Buddhism was about reaching enlightenment, but I assumed this was all just marketing. I never signed on for any kind of philosophical journey or spiritual growth. I only ever wanted a good night's sleep. I kept meditating because the only other options were to recontinue my medication or go back to wandering around my neighbourhood late at night, hallucinating.

I had friends who meditated and when I asked them about it (with feigned casualness) they explained that they sat for five minutes before bedtime when they'd had a bad day, or went on a retreat every year or so, and they found it pleasant and relaxing but nothing more than that. My neurochemistry seemed to be broken in ways that required a deeper practice to have much effect, and that level of commitment kept prodding me, gently but persistently, towards further strange experiences and discomforting insights.

I didn't tell many people what I was experiencing. The whole thing was embarrassing. But at the same time it was novel and interesting. As you get older it becomes harder to surprise yourself, and to find myself in my mid-forties sitting cross-legged on a cushion every day, occasionally experiencing visions and states of pure tranquillity, was new and surprising. But it took me about a year to get over my irritation and embarrassment and accept that I was now progressing down a path I never chose, and start to wonder where it led.

The Valley and the Stream

On the third night I woke to find my body filled with a strange energy. It felt like soda water fizzing beneath my skin. At first I was excited. I sat up in my bed and wondered what would happen next. But nothing happened next. The energy didn't go away or change. It was just there. After about twenty minutes I was bored. I wondered how long it would last. It was midnight and in five hours' time someone would bang a gong outside my door. Then I would rise, drink tea in the communal kitchen with the other guests—in silence; this was a silent retreat—and then we'd march uphill through the rain and dripping trees to the meditation hall, a classroom-sized room with bare wooden floors, white plaster walls, and windows looking out over a deep valley. We'd meditate for two hours, then break for breakfast, then sit for another two and a half hours, then two more hours in the afternoon and one in the evening. I knew that if I didn't sleep I'd spend most of the next day dozing or daydreaming instead of meditating. A whole day of my five-day retreat wasted. I lay on my back, seething. When, I wondered, steepling my fingers and drumming them against my chest, would this mystical experience end? I tried to relax. I focused on my breathing. Eventually I fell asleep.

I woke feeling normal. I got up, drank my tea and formed one of the vague shadows moving through the pre-dawn dark up the trail to the hall. Someone had already lit the fire. The rain was steady on the roof. We sat cross-legged on mats or wooden meditation stools or chairs, with blankets draped around our shoulders. Our teacher chanted in Tibetan while the rest of us mumbled along. Then we meditated. About forty minutes in, I was alert but calm—no thoughts, no distractions—when I perceived an object in my mind, hovering at the periphery of my awareness. It was a greenish-gold colour, like iridescent scales. It had a high musical tone, a vaguely circular shape. I switched my attention to it and it amplified, slowly at first then quickly: a rogue algorithm, looping, asymptotic, exploding inside my mind and pulsing off and on, a strobing effect blotting out all self-awareness, all other sensations. It was both pleasurable and frightening. I had no conception of my body yet at the same time I felt like I was falling, faster and faster. I couldn't breathe.

*

What is enlightenment? It's still not clear to me. In traditional Buddhism, it's linked to the pre-Buddhist Hindu belief in karma and reincarnation. Enlightenment is how you escape the endless cosmic cycle of suffering and rebirth. But most contemporary Buddhists seem to prefer the term 'awakening', the metaphor being that we're all asleep and don't know it, and this confused state is—allegedly—the cause of our suffering. When we wake to the true nature of reality, the suffering ceases, revealing a nameless, unimaginable form of freedom—a new perception of existence, some state beyond words.

There's a lot of—mostly—amicable disagreement about what awakening is like and whether anyone has ever really achieved it. Some argue that there are multiple stages of awakening, like levels in a video game; others say that awakening is just an ideal, something to aspire to in your meditation practice but which you can never really reach.

There's more consensus around the *jhanas*, the alternate states of consciousness that precede and point towards awakening. The story goes like this: when the Buddha was a young man he left home to become a mystic. He studied under several spiritual masters who taught him yoga and meditation and these skills allowed him to access the jhanas. If you reach a deep enough level of concentration, you can access these progressively sublime and indescribable mental states, and the way you think and experience the world literally changes.

There are four jhanas, or maybe eight depending on who you ask. You enter them sequentially, and each requires a higher level of meditative skill to access. The Buddha reached the highest jhana, but was still dissatisfied, still not awakened, so he sat beneath a tree (the Bodhi tree, now a famous pilgrimage site) and vowed not to move until he achieved awakening. He did this, the scriptures claim, by going beyond the jhanas and perceiving the three characteristics of existence, deep insights into the true nature of reality.

Awakening is mysterious, but the jhanas are a real thing. Lots of people experience them and have done for thousands of years. The *Digha Nikaya* ('The Collection of Long Discourses'), one of the scriptures in the Pāli Canon, the oldest extant Buddhist texts, describes the first jhana: 'Quite secluded from sense pleasures, secluded from unwholesome states of mind, he enters and dwells in the first jhana, which is accompanied by applied thought and sustained thought with rapture and happiness born of seclusion. One drenches, steeps, saturates and suffuses one's body with this rapture and happiness.'

This sounded good to me, and about a year into my meditation practice I started to follow the instructions to jhana access. But being secluded from sense pleasures and unwholesome states of mind is hard work. Or, rather, it is hard work to get to the point where it no longer feels like hard work, which is the point you need to reach.

You need sustained and effortless access concentration in order to enter the jhanas, and here is where we meet the famously paradoxical nature of meditation: if you want to achieve a jhana state, you can't. Only by not wanting it can you obtain it. The way this worked for me is that I meditated for hours until I finally found myself in a calm, thoughtless state, effortlessly focused on the breath, and then my mind blared, 'I'm doing it! I'm so calm and focused!', shattering my equanimity and flooding my thoughts with feelings of disappointment, frustration and exasperation, which are of course additionally destabilising.

I persevered. But I still couldn't enter the jhanas. I felt blocked. I had weird pulses of energy in my hands during the day. At night I experienced a fluttering in my mind, like something trying to batter its way free. I wasn't relaxed enough, the texts suggested. My main source for studying jhana practice—Leigh Brasington's *Right Concentration: A Practical Guide to the Jhanas*—explained that it is hard for people living in the day-to-day world to access these states. You just don't get the seclusion and calm you need for the enterprise. The Buddha himself provided advice on where to go for jhana practise. Avoid large or new monasteries, he counselled. Frontiers, ports and haunted places are also bad. Instead he recommended secluded dwellings, caves, clefts in cliffs. Cemeteries. And mountains.

The Wangapeka Study and Retreat Centre sits on the higher slopes of a large hill, arguably a small mountain, in the northern foothills of the Southern Alps. You reach it via a long and winding dirt road leading to a steep and winding dirt driveway, leading to a carpark and then a series of dirt trails through the trees. There are huts and campsites scattered about the clearings. Some of them have 'Retreat in Progress' signs posted on barriers blocking entry to their trails. These are occupied by solo retreatants: people who've been up there for months, meditating alone.

The main building, midway up the hillside, houses the kitchen, toilets and showers, and a large communal space that functions as a combination of dining room, meeting room and library. French doors open out onto a rectangular lawn where you can practise yoga or tai chi, if you are so inclined, which almost everyone who would stay at a place like Wangapeka is. At right angles to the main building is a row of narrow, cell-like guest rooms, the third of which was mine.

The centre was founded in 1975, and was built up gradually over the years by members of the community—mostly New Zealand Buddhists who followed the Tibetan tradition and lived in the region, of which there were surprisingly many—hauling wooden beams and bags of concrete mix up the slopes, clearing trees, hacking pathways through the bush.

There was a map of the hill posted in the foyer of the main building. It claimed to show all of these pathways, including routes to a lookout, a waterfall, a pagoda and a swimming hole. The retreat schedule allowed the guests a few hours of free time each day and I spent most of mine attempting to find these locations, but the map was decades out of date, so I always got lost. I wandered between the pines and tangles of wild blackberry, the long wet grass of the trails soaking my shoes, socks and trackpants up to my knees. Sometimes I encountered other equally lost wanderers, also on retreat. None of us were allowed to talk so we always shrugged theatrically and mimed a stream or waterfall: whatever we'd found, and the direction we'd found it. Pagodas are hard to mime.

On the third day, the day before I reached the first jhana, I found the lookout: a clearing on the north side of the hill. Far below it were farmlands—asymmetric light and dark green fields, the Wangapeka River winding between them, disappearing into a distant haze of sunlit mist. The fields were flanked by pine-covered hills, steep slopes of forest broken by cliffs, waterfalls spilling into the air, low clouds interrupted by columns of light.

I was in a philosophical mood. Partly it was all that silence and alpine air, but also it was having spent the months before the retreat trying to read *Being and Time*, a dense, often incomprehensible book by Martin Heidegger, who wrote extensively about anxiety and depression.

All through his life Heidegger tried to understand the problem of Being. Everything I saw from the lookout—the hills, the river, the light—existed in the world; they were all entities instantiated in space-time, and although they were all different, Heidegger pointed out that they all shared the same mysterious property of existence. What was this property? What was Being? How is it that we are part of the world, made up of the same matter and energy as everything else, but also able to observe it?

He felt that these questions lay outside the boundaries of rationality. They could never be explained by studying, say, physics or psychology. The sciences can explain the world of facts, he conceded, and there is nothing supernatural within the world they cannot describe. But sometimes, in moments of deep thought, or depressed or anxious moods, the world of facts and language seems like a thin membrane stretched over the unknowable true nature of things. We barely know what we really are and we barely know that we do not know. His philosophy depicts the world as a dark and endless forest in which humans are clearings in space and time, where existence suddenly opens up, glimpsing itself, and Being briefly emerges into the light.

*

Mood obviously has something to do with neurotransmitters: tiny chemical messengers that interact with neurons, the hundred-billion-odd branch-like elongated cells that make up our nervous system. The most famous neurotransmitter is serotonin, a fairly small, simple molecule. If you tell your doctor you have depression or anxiety they'll probably prescribe an SSRI: a Selective Serotonin Reuptake Inhibitor, a class of drug that increases the extracellular levels of serotonin in key regions of your brain, and which sometimes improves mood and sometimes does not, for reasons nobody yet understands.

The scientific debate on SSRIs is very heated. Some studies find they're an effective treatment for depression and anxiety, others that they're almost indistinguishable from placebos. Back in my late thirties, when my doctor first diagnosed me and wrote out a prescription, I'd already spent hours reading the clinical literature on antidepressants and obsessing over anti-pharmacology conspiracy websites. I explained all of my doubts about the drugs in between bouts of exhausted weeping. 'Try them anyway,' my doctor advised. 'All I know is that they definitely help some people.' So I tried them and they helped me.

We know the chemical structure of serotonin and the rest of the monoamine class of neurotransmitters that are linked to mood disorders. We know how they're metabolised and transported around the brain. We know how they interact with our neurons. What no one understands is how all of this biochemical activity affects the experience of subjective consciousness. Why does serotonin make you happy? How does it affect mood? What is mood? What is depression? How does any of this stuff work?

Philosophers refer to these questions and the debate around them as 'the hard problem of consciousness'. If you're standing in a room and the room gets colder, a thermometer will measure the drop in temperature as the liquid inside it contracts as it cools. But humans and other species *feel* the drop in temperature. We have an internal, subjective experience of being cold. Our brains create this feeling, along with other feelings of pain, happiness, sadness, joy, etc., which philosophers refer to as qualia. But no one knows how the brain does this, or what the neurons are doing that is so profoundly different from thermometers and all the other matter in the universe. To put it another way: how could we reverse engineer consciousness and build a thermometer that *feels* the cold? Where would you start? Consciousness seems to be a property of the universe that everyone is familiar with—it is, if you want to get deep, the only thing we're ever familiar with—but which is hard to even think about, let alone investigate scientifically.

Some philosophers say that the hard problem can never be solved (Heidegger would say it can never be *rationally* solved) or that the failure of biologists to solve it means that evolutionary theory is incomplete, possibly wrong. Others 'solve' it by declaring that consciousness is an illusion and that therefore there is no problem to solve. The psychologist Susan

Blackmore points out, 'An illusion is not something that does not exist [. . .] Rather, it is something that it is not what it appears to be.' So even if there is an illusion, there is still a phenomenon to be explained.

Others insist that the question itself is incoherent and that by stating this they have solved the mystery. (Ever since Wittgenstein, it has been fashionable for philosophers to announce they've solved a problem by restating it in a formal language that proves it doesn't exist.) It's all a very lively debate. But from my perspective, depression feels like something is wrong with my consciousness. The way I experience the world is broken. Even if this is all just an illusion, it would be nice to know how the trick works, and why it fails.

*

There were about twenty fellow guests on my retreat and everyone had a job to do. Some people helped prepare the meals. Others cleaned. I washed the dishes after dinner. I resented this when I read about it in the booking confirmation email. 'I'm paying these people money to wash dishes?' But when you see the system in action it makes sense. A group meditation retreat is a very weird social situation: you're living in close proximity with a bunch of strangers, but you're not allowed to talk to them. The job system means social bonding still happens because everyone does things for each other, little reciprocal chores. So you feel like you're part of a community, but there's no gossip or status anxiety because there's no conversation.

When I told my friends about the retreat they fixated on the commitment to five days of silence, wondering how anyone could stand it. I looked forward to it. I'm an introverted person, and this manifests as a sense of unease in most social situations. The unease is usually faint, a buzzing at the edge of my mind, easy to ignore, but if there are too many people around me the unease builds. Then I feel uneasy about feeling uneasy. Crowded pubs are stressful, as are buses and trains. Concerts. Airports. My daughter's ballet school when all the classes change and I am surrounded by dense flocks of small girls dressed in pink, and their parents and bored siblings, all yelling at each other while my family yells at me. In these situations the buzzing amplifies, drowning out everything else, and all I want to do is get away.

This introversion tips me towards unsociability. I don't eat lunch with my workmates. If I have the choice between going out at night and staying in, I stay in. And even when I'm at home with my family, my inclination is to go into another room and read a book or look at the internet. At the same time I have a deep compulsion towards distraction, a dread of boredom. My mind always wants to be occupied, by a book or social media or a video game. Anything. There's an infamous psychological study from 2014 in which people were given electric shocks then asked if they were willing to pay money not to be shocked a second time. If they offered to pay because they really hated being shocked, they were left alone in the room with the electroshock equipment still wired up, and over half of them—predominantly men—deliberately shocked themselves out of boredom.

I am very much part of this shock-yourself-for-no-reason demographic. Whenever I sit and meditate, a part of my mind screams at me that I have to open my eyes, have to go and do something, anything other than just sit and be quiet. I associate my depression with these two traits: introversion and distraction. I want to be alone but then I feel lonely, and I want to be distracted but then my brain feels overwhelmed. So I found it interesting that the mindfulness retreat seemed designed to prohibit exactly this pattern of behaviour. Distraction was banned and the environment was communal but minimally social. You weren't lonely, but you were stuck with yourself and your thoughts.

When we first arrived at the retreat we were allowed to talk to each other, and the question most people asked me was 'How long have you followed Jakob?' Jakob was the teacher. He ran the retreat, and people were surprised to learn that I didn't follow him, or even know who he was. 'He was a student of Dilgo Khyentse Rinpoche,' they explained in hushed tones, naming one of the most revered figures in Tibetan Buddhism, a teacher of the current Dalai Lama, but I didn't know who Dilgo Khyentse Rinpoche was either.

Jakob was a lean ponytailed Norwegian in, I guessed, his late fifties or early sixties, based on his comments about backpacking around India as a teenager in the early seventies. He looked younger; his meditation posture was an effortless lotus. He gave us hour-long dharma talks every night. We could approach him whenever we had a question about his teachings, and each of us had a brief, scheduled meeting with him to discuss our spiritual progress.

My meeting took place in the Octagon. This was a small building just down the hill from the main lawn. It consisted of a single empty room with nothing on the walls, and windows looking out into a bank of white fog. Jakob waited inside, sitting on a chair in the centre of the room. He asked me about his talks. Did I understand everything?

This was awkward. I'd booked the retreat without knowing anything about the different strands of Buddhism, assuming any teacher could answer all my questions about jhanas, but on the first night Jakob had explained that jhanas weren't part of the Tibetan tradition he followed. 'It's not my job to dangle alternate states of awareness in front of you,' he'd said, before going on to tell us about lamas and reincarnation and higher realms of existence.

But I'd come on this retreat to try and access the jhanas, so during the meditation sessions I followed my own practice and ignored all of Jakob's advice. This seemed like a rude thing to say to his face, so instead I asked him about consciousness and the hard problem, subjects that had been much on my mind. This was partly Martin Heidegger's fault, but on retreat you do nothing but consider the self, and you inevitably wonder what you are observing, and what you're observing it with.

'Buddhism believes that consciousness is primary,' Jakob replied. 'Consciousness creates the material world.'

'But the brain obviously creates consciousness,' I replied. 'How could consciousness precede the material world when it's created by it?'

'Is the conscious mind created by the brain?' Jakob asked, smiling the smile of someone who is both filled with wisdom and loving compassion, and aware that he is about to kick someone's ass in a spiritual debate. 'How does it do that?'

I didn't have an answer to this question. Nobody does. But I didn't worry about it for the rest of the retreat, because I didn't worry about anything. I meditated. I stared at trees and clouds. I woke at night pulsing with energy. I felt astonished by the presence of Being. On the fourth morning I accessed the first jhana, felt my skull flood with light, fell out about twenty seconds later, and spent the rest of the day stabilising the state, resting in an uncomplicated mode of pure bliss. I spent my spare time walking the trails, feeling the bliss echo and reverberate inside my deliciously empty mind. I stopped at the sealed-off paths leading to the self-retreat cabins and wondered what it felt like inside the heads of the people who'd been up there for months.

But I thought about Jakob's question on the flight home and I thought about it some more back at work where, after a day or two, all of the effects of the retreat evaporated and I felt identical to how I'd felt before I left. I meditated for hours in the early mornings and tried to access the jhana again but failed, gave up, and went back to my rudimentary half-an-hour-a-day practice.

I read essays and papers on cognitive psychology and neuroscience. The field was entering a golden age—staggering technological breakthroughs pointing to a grand unified theory of human cognition. This theory went by several names: predictive coding, or predictive processing, or the free energy principle. It was complex, highly mathematical and way beyond my comprehension. But it pointed towards the things I was interested in, like explanations of mood, mood disorders, tentative solutions to the hard problem, and an answer to Jakob's question. When the summer rolled around and my university closed down for Christmas, I printed out a pile of neuroscience papers and took them on holiday with me.

We rented a place by the sea in Waikanae, the spiritual and geographic opposite of Wangapeka: a low-lying labyrinth of malls, golf courses, luxury car dealerships and retirement villages, all repeating with such regularity it seemed randomly generated, as if you could go on driving past the beaches and expressway on-ramps forever. Instead of meditating in the early mornings I walked along the beach, following the maze of paths through the sand dunes. Sometimes I wrapped myself in a blanket and sat outside on a recliner to read my predictive processing papers while the sun rose. Other mornings I just sat and looked at the sea. I started to feel both anxious and weirdly anticipatory about climate change. I fantasised about storm surges obliterating the baches and mansions arranged along the curve of the coast. I stopped meditating altogether. What was the point? And when the holiday was over and I was back at work, I found myself waking in the middle of the night, every night, and my depression settled in again.

Once when my daughter was a baby I hid her favourite toy behind my back. I didn't know that you played this game with older babies but not young ones, because young babies don't have object permanence. They assume that anything vanishing from their visual field no longer exists. As soon as the toy—I think it was a pig—was out of sight she started screaming.

A newly formed baby's brain is a complex biochemical-electrical goo encased inside a small but expanding skull. It doesn't understand much about the world, but there's a constant stream of sense data—light, movement, smell, sound, touch, taste. It is far more information than can possibly be processed. The brain's job is to take that torrent of data and build an accurate model of reality, so that as the baby grows it can navigate the world, move its body around in it, evade predators, find food and mates, survive amidst the deluge of information.

The way we do that, according to the predictive processing model of cognition, is by generating predictions and matching them against our sense data. If someone sticks their finger in a baby's face, its brain will wonder: will this object feel solid if I touch it, or will my hand simply pass through it? The brain makes a prediction about how something will feel, look, sound or behave, then it tests the prediction against the incoming signal. If the prediction is validated, the assumptions behind it

44

are built into the brain's model ('visible things feel solid') and used to generate more predictions: 'Given that this person's finger is solid, will it taste good if I put it in my mouth and bite it really hard?' This is why children like the same stories and games and experiences repeated over and over. If you're building a model of reality based on prediction, you want the same datasets to fine-tune against. Humans have a much longer period of childhood than any other species, suggesting our predictive models are far more complex.

A few weeks after we got back from the beach holiday I was at home alone, feeling sleep-deprived and depressed. I walked from the unlit hallway into my bedroom and saw a very tall woman in old-fashioned clothes standing with her back to me, backlit by the window. It was very frightening. It also wasn't real, just a suit jacket hanging from the curtain rail with the afternoon sun behind it.

Our brains never stop making predictions ('the bedroom will be empty') and matching them against the information our senses obtain about the world. If the prediction fails ('There's an impossibly tall woman in my room!'), it generates an error and places the brain in a state of statistical uncertainty. The brain hates this. Predictive processing argues that all human behaviour can be framed in terms of reducing error and uncertainty. If you walk into a dark room, it's really hard for your brain to predict what's inside it, so your immediate impulse is to turn on the light, because that makes it easier to check your predictions. And we don't notice that our brain is constantly revising its predictions, because it conceals this process from our conscious awareness. A few days ago I was driving through the countryside and saw something in my peripheral vision: a dark object moving through a field. I turned to look at it, and saw, for a split second, a black lamb, then a black horse, and then the object stabilised as a human in a black jacket, along with the overwhelming impression that it had always been a human in a black jacket, that I hadn't seen anything else. (Having the clarity to catch these little revisions as they happen is one of the dubious benefits of concentration meditation.)

Once we have a robust model of reality that seems to match the the world around us—meaning, it generates predictions with minimal error—our brains can filter out all the the irrelevant data the the world saturates it with. We have a model of language processing, for example, and one of the the predictions it makes is that the the multiple repeats of the word 'the' in this paragraph are errors, so it strips them out before presenting them to conscious awareness. And we often don't notice the the sound of the air conditioning in an office, or the the traffic on distant roads, or other low-information noise because, again, our model of reality assumes it has no value. We might hear it now, or see redundant words if my mentioning these things means that the the prior assumptions have been temporarily challenged, but after a few minutes they disappear again.

The result of all this computation and filtering is the phenomenal world: the sequence of predictions that plays out inside our minds. When we wave our hands in front of our face, the image is happening inside our skulls. Our brains have no direct access to reality but, starting from nothing, they've constructed a detailed, controlled hallucination, calibrating it against changes in air pressure translated into sound, streams of electromagnetic radiation into images, sense data into touch. Even when we take action in the world, the brain makes a prediction—'I will scratch my nose'—and the body moves the arm, hand and fingers to make the prediction come true. All we ever encounter is prediction upon prediction, the exquisitely calibrated hallucination; and all we ever feel, all our joy and pain and sadness, is a fluctuating measure of uncertainty about the statistical accuracy of the model.

It always starts with the insomnia. This isn't so bad, at first. My bed is comfortable, and I never feel like I have enough time in the day just to think, so when I wake at 1am with inane thoughts and snatches of a song looping around my head I try to stay calm. If it is summer and the curtains are open I can see the tops of trees and the night sky and sometimes the stars. I pass the time by writing things in my head, or making plans for the future, or litigating arguments with my enemies on the internet. I take great care not to disturb my wife, and so long as I stay absolutely still and breathe regularly I am fairly safe. I feel awful the next day and always assume I'll sleep well that night, but I wake up at 1am again. It only takes a few days of this before I realise I'm no longer tired; I'm depressed.

Depression is not always depressing. Sadness is not the default state. I mean, yes, sometimes you're sad, but the classic symptom of clinical depression (and remember, no one knows what these diseases are; all we have are symptoms) is anhedonia: the inability to experience pleasure. Plath famously compared it to being trapped under a bell jar, walled off from the rest of the world. You feel nothing, and it sounds paradoxical but feeling nothing feels horrible.

I'm now familiar with the behavioural markers of anxiety and depression, at least in myself. The insomnia. The obsessional looping: the same thoughts, usually negative, self-critical, over and over again. I become withdrawn and antisocial, even more than normal. I want to stay inside with the lights off and the curtains drawn and binge-watch TV. I become irritable and selfish, even more than normal. I'm indecisive. I cry over trivial things, and during the post-beach holiday depressive episode I found myself blinking back tears one day when I tried to cross a busy road and there were no gaps in the traffic. I attempted to meditate but even though I could lie in bed watching sitcoms for hours I couldn't concentrate on my breath for more than thirty seconds. I went back on antidepressants. This always feels like a miserable defeat and it always works. I felt better. I started meditating again and slowly tapered off the drugs. This took about two months.

*

Karl Friston, the world's most-cited living neuroscientist, is the researcher most closely associated with predictive processing. When Friston was eight years old he spent a summer's afternoon watching insects scurry around in his back garden in suburban England, trying to understand the purpose behind their activity. At first he thought they were seeking shelter and darkness because they spent more time in the shade, but then he realised this was selection bias. The insects in the sun moved faster than those in the shade because they were energised by the warmth. There was no purpose. The insect's behaviour was just random.

Scientists prefer explanations that are parsimonious. They try to see the deep simplicity behind the apparent complexity of the world. Friston and other champions of predictive processing are excited by their theory because it explains so many diverse features of the brain that otherwise seem mysterious. What does consciousness do? What does the imagination do? Why do we sleep? What are dreams? What is mood and why do so many people have mood disorders?

The question of what consciousness *does* is not the 'hard

problem', which demands to know how consciousness works. Instead it addresses a related debate about why consciousness even exists. What purpose does it serve for us to be able to 'feel' the cold instead of just registering it in some physical state, like a thermometer? To talk about this problem, philosophers invented a thought experiment: the famous philosophical zombie, or p-zombie.

The p-zombie does not look like a horror movie zombie. It looks and behaves exactly like a normal human. The only difference is that it has no consciousness. It experiences the cold in the exact same manner as a thermometer. A lot of human cognition takes place out of reach of our conscious awareness. While you're reading this your brain is regulating your heart rate, blood sugar, oxygen levels, and countless other physiological states, and it's making corrections, occasionally sending signals to your conscious mind telling you to eat something, or urinate, or go to sleep. You have no executive access to any of that information. You can't shut your eyes and estimate your blood gas levels, but if your brain stopped measuring and regulating them you'd die very quickly.

All of this activity, Friston claims, consists of the brain making predictions about the body's internal states and then minimising error between the prediction and the data. A p-zombie's brain works the same way, only there's no subjective awareness at all.

Two figures meet in a clearing. One is a human. The other is a p-zombie. They both 'see' a snake in the grass, but the human *sees* the snake in the same way all of us visualise the external world inside our own heads. The human feels afraid, screams and runs away. But the p-zombie doesn't see or feel anything. Instead the image of the snake is projected onto its retina. The visual information is processed by the brain in the same unconscious autonomic way our brains process information about blood gas. It identifies the snake, matching it to images stored in memory associated with information about danger and threat, instructs the mouth and lungs to scream to alert anyone nearby, and issues more instructions to its skeletal and muscular system to turn and run away. There is never any fear, or any feeling or thought at all, only a flow of chemistry and light and information.

Back in the nineteenth century, the biologist T.H. Huxley took great delight in declaring that consciousness was an 'epiphenomenon': a pointless by-product of cognition, like exhaust from a car. Our awareness of our lives was, he claimed, 'like the bell of a clock that has no role in keeping the time'. This was an amusingly shocking thing for Huxley to announce at public lectures in the late Victorian age, to audiences who felt consciousness was bound up with human exceptionalism and our immortal souls. But he had no proof for his claim and it seems not to be true. The consciousness of living creatures exists in layers of sophistication and complexity, the simplest of which are evolutionarily ancient, which suggests that consciousness is doing something vital in terms of natural selection.

The Portuguese-American neuroscientist Antonio Damasio identifies the seat of subjective consciousness in the brain stem, a primordial component of the nervous system. Maybe this is absurd, but I'm troubled by the idea of consciousness emerging long before the development of communication; that most of life on Earth consisted of aeons of sentient creatures awakening in the warm oceans, thrown into existence with no way to connect, living and dying alone, repeated trillions of times. This is the sort of thing I think about when I wake at 1am.

*

I grew up in a valley in the suburbs. Lots of families there had dogs, including ours, and sometimes a dog would start barking and all the other dogs would bark back, back and forth across the valley, then people would yell at the dogs, and more dogs would bark at them. This could go on for hours.

The Mind Illuminated—one of the most popular secular Buddhist texts—presents a model of consciousness drawn from the Yogacara school, a Buddhist philosophical tradition dating from the second to the fourth century CE. Like all good philosophers, the Yogacarins were interested in the nature of perception and cognition, and they argued that the reality presented to us in the mind is just a representation of the real (which aligns to the predictive processing claim that it's all just a calibrated hallucination). But they also argued that the mind is modular—that instead of a single, unified self, it consists of many separate components, or subminds.

This is something that becomes apparent when I meditate. I sit and close my eyes because part of me wants to, but then another part of my mind wants me to get up and go do something else. I try to concentrate on the breath. My mind wanders. I bring it back. It wanders again. This is boring but, the Buddhists claim, it's teaching us something profound: that there is no single, unified self. Consciousness is merely a way for the separate subminds to communicate with each other. All of our decisions are made at a subconscious level and then broadcast to consciousness. Sometimes the subminds disagree and we feel indecisive. Sometimes they clash, violently, and we feel torn. But our consciousness is only ever a witness, a screen for subminds to project thoughts onto. It has no agency. There's no free will, no soul, no indivisible self.

Restated in the language of modern neuroscience, the brain consists of linked, large-scale networks, and consciousness is a global workspace for them to share predictions and responses. So one component—probably the fronto-parietal network, roughly the upper back part of the brain, which is associated with goal-driven behaviour and executive planning—decides to meditate and tries to focus on the breath. It frames this as a prediction and broadcasts it so the rest of the brain knows which movements to make to minimise the uncertainty and make the prediction come true. But when I sit and kneel and close my eyes, another component, probably the default mode network, a module involved in thinking about the past and predicting the future, activates and broadcasts its own inane, pointless thoughts, over and over, and then other networks— memories, emotions—respond to them. A non-mystical way to describe the early, frustrating period of learning to meditate is that you're training all of these networks to shut up and stop barking at each other.

So the fourth-century Buddhist reply to the twenty-first-century problem of the p-zombie is that the zombie's behaviour is different from the human's. When the p-zombie sees the snake it doesn't scream and run away, at least not with the speed and computational efficiency of a human. The zombie's visual system can't broadcast the snake's presence to the rest of the mind all at once, for the simple reason that there's nothing to broadcast it to. Consciousness isn't purposeless, as Huxley suggested, but we don't have it because we're lit with an essence of the divine spark, as the priests and intellectuals he argued with claimed. We're conscious because it's more computationally efficient.

When I was wandering the trails at Wangapeka my brain attempted to understand how the maze of forks and branches matched with the partial map of trails in my memory. When I found the lookout I felt happiness: the brain's way of rewarding the subminds for accurate predictions. If I wound up at a dead end I felt sadness, frustration. The subminds' models were wrong. Predictive processing sees emotions as responses to events which increase or decrease uncertainty.

But what is mood? Why do we experience sustained feelings of happiness or anxiety or sadness? Why don't we just exist in a transient stream of pleasure and pain? Friston's answer is that moods are high-level priors, meaning that they're predictions about the accuracy of your emotional responses. If we're wandering through the forest and keep hitting dead ends despite dozens of attempts, we feel anger at each failure and after a while we feel a more persistent sour mood, which is a way of signalling to the subminds that whatever they're doing, it isn't working. Then we might succeed, once, and find our way to a branch that looks familiar. But the brain doesn't want us to feel happy and tell the subminds that their predictive models are correct, because they probably aren't. If we've been wrong dozens of times in a row and right only once, it's probably just by chance. Bad moods attenuate those signals of happiness.

And if this prior gets stuck in place for a long period of time you're anhedonic, i.e. you're never happy, i.e. you're depressed. Predictive processing suggests that depression is a persistent prior predicting bad outcomes with high confidence. This prior says that we're always on the wrong path, always heading towards a dead end. When something goes wrong the prior is validated, but when things go right the feelings of happiness or joy are suppressed, because the prior assumes anything good is just statistical noise.

Anxiety happens when the brain predicts bad outcomes with low confidence, and this accounts for that disorder's classic symptom: obsessional looping. Subminds repeatedly project the same thoughts into consciousness, hoping to reduce error. In the lost-in-the-forest analogy, we think the path ahead simply leads back to where we're standing right now but we're not sure, so we take it, but when we come to this spot again we still aren't sure, so we take it again. And again. And again.

Many of the contemporary theories about mood disorders involve genetics, epigenetics, diet, inflammation, environment, stress, early childhood development—really complicated combinations of all of these really complicated things. But there's one subject that often crops up in the mood disorder literature and that is highly relevant to predictive processing and meaningful to my own experience. Sleep and sleep deprivation.

Sleep has always annoyed biologists. Evolution is supposed to be this ruthless struggle for existence, but every day most complex organisms stop competing for mates and eating each other. Instead they lie down and shut their eyes and ignore everything around them for *hours*. Sleep should get heavily selected against. We know alternatives to deep sleep are possible. Look at the unihemispheric sleep behaviour of dolphins: the different sides of their brains take turns to sleep so the creatures can keep swimming in the right direction over long distances. And yet deep sleep and dreaming are the norm among complex land animals. Why?

Sleep seems to do a number of important things, and many of them involve computational complexity. If I'm in the maze of trails trying to find my way back to my room, I might pick paths by flipping a coin. I know there's a 50 per cent chance it'll come up heads, 50 per cent tails, but even if I don't know this I could figure it out just by flipping the coin a number of times and observing the results. In other words, I'd build a predictive model. In theory it would be easy to remember this model and make predictions using it, because it's so simple. 50/50. Heads or tails.

But let's say there's some noise in my coin flips and it comes up heads slightly more often than tails. There's nothing wrong with the coin, it's just dumb random chance. Existence is full of it. But because my brain is a predictive processor I have to update my model of how the coin behaves, and try to remember there's a 0.51 probability I'll flip heads and an 0.49 probability I'll flip tails. And as I move around I notice something else. If I flip a coin when I'm facing uphill, it's slightly more likely to come up tails than if I'm facing downhill. Again, this doesn't mean anything. It's just more noise, but now I have to update my model again, and it's getting more complex. And this goes on and on, all day every day. Every prediction and outcome adds more noise to my operating models of the world. It gets harder to store them, and to make predictions based on them, and none of the complication adds any value to my predictive accuracy. It only takes about sixteen hours for my models of reality to become pointlessly complex and expensive. What I need is a process to strip out all that noise.

Every night we sleep and our overly complicated model of the world goes offline. It's still making predictions but, unless we have a serious sleep disorder, we can't move our bodies to match up with them, and there's very little sense data coming in. These predictions are dreams. They seem to 'prune redundancy and reduce complexity', as Friston puts it. My hypothetical model for coin flips gets reset to a simple 50/50. And when I'm not suffering from depression, this process resets all those high-level mood priors. If I have a terrible day I sleep on it, and wake feeling fine.

If you meditate for long enough you see and experience a lot of strange things. I've had visions, heard voices, felt bizarre bodily sensations. They're a lot like dreams, but I experience them with total clarity because I'm not asleep. My mind is making predictions, because that's what it does, but when I'm deep in a meditative state it doesn't have any external data to match against. I haven't had an out-of-body experience yet, but I've lost all connection with my senses a few times. Both phenomena seem to connect to a brain region called the temporoparietal junction, which integrates sense data, and which is probably doing something odd when people have the common meditative experience that they've floated out of their body and into some higher realm of being, or glimpsed another plane of existence.

*

After the jhana, I spent the afternoon walking around the trails. I found some of the trees I liked and just stared at them, delighted that entities of such beauty could exist, manifesting themselves into the world out of nothing. I felt extremely sane. While walking slowly between pines I noticed something in my peripheral vision. It was a weka, a sleek flightless brown-feathered bird, standing about knee height, staring at me from the foliage. We contemplated each other for a few moments, me drinking in the animal's wet beauty, it probably wondering whether I was likely to chase it down and eat it. I felt sorry for the weka, which would probably end up being killed by a dog, or some other carnivore, against which its evolution on a remote island with no mammalian predators left it defenceless.

Then I thought: wasn't I in a similar position to the weka? Wasn't I operating outside my own evolutionary niche? True, I wasn't in danger of being eaten by dogs. Instead my brain was optimised for low information, high risk, high opportunity environments. But I lived in a leafy suburb and worked at a university, and they were the exact opposite: high information, low risk. I spent every day trying to absorb as much data as I could, reading emails and books and papers, scrolling social media, the news, TV. I did this because my brain thought it was important to form an accurate model of reality and to be alert to risk, like the sleek little weka detecting potential predators. But for me there were no risks and my culture saturated me in an infinite amount of information, which overloaded my brain and made me sick. 'I am the weka,' I murmured into the silence of the clearing. The actual weka had already vanished into the ferns.

I thought about all of this again on my beach holiday, reading my neuroscience papers, following trails of footprints across the wet sand. I realised that all of the information I'm drenched with, addicted to, adds noise to my models of reality and generates a huge amount of self-referential chatter between my subminds. This is especially so if I'm spending a lot of time on the internet, interacting with content designed to make me feel anxious or outraged or angry. And, like the dogs from my childhood, pointlessly barking at each other across the valley, this internal chatter has a looping, cumulative effect— information generating information, noise amplifying noise. I forget most of it when I sleep and this gives my life an odd, amnesiac-like quality. Every day I try to learn what's going on in the world, and every night I forget almost everything.

Friston doesn't go into a lot of detail in his paper on dreaming. How does it 'prune and simplify' our models of reality? He doesn't say. I am not a neuroscientist, nor an expert on brain imaging, or any kind of expert at all. I'm just a depressive who had a blissful green light explode inside his head.

But the way I imagine it works is that the sleeping mind generates a thought—some memory or fantasy or nightmare—

designed to provoke a specific response, then it measures the actual reaction and prunes out all the priors that deviate from the prediction or that make no measurable difference. You have a bad day and go to bed angry, then you have a flying dream and your mind strips out everything that inhibits the predicted response of happiness and elation. And the narrative component of our consciousness strings all these unrelated predictions together, which gives us the weird, nonlinear, non-logical dream narrative, and that's why hours and hours of uncontrolled hallucinations cause us to wake up feeling normal.

Unless, that is, your brain is so overstimulated, so drowned in information that you wake in the night with your subminds screaming nonsense at each other. If healthy sustained sleep doesn't happen then none of the pruning takes place; none of the high-level mood priors get reset. So day by day we feel a little more exhausted because we're trying to make sense of the world with these noisy, computationally expensive models of reality, and our overall mood becomes a sinking lid. It never gets reset. We're stuck in a depressive state.

For me, this model of depression explains a lot. It explains why insomnia is so closely tied to my depressive episodes. It explains why I want to sit in a dark room and binge-watch the same old TV shows. I'm minimising uncertainty. And it explains why meditation helps treat the disorder. It's significant, I think, that concentration meditation deals exclusively with simple repetitive subjects: the breath, a mantra, the flame of a candle. Nothing to complicate the models. I think this disrupts the obsessional looping that's so characteristic of mood disorders, which keeps those high-level priors stuck on depressive or anxious modes. And, at the same time, I'm training my mind to ignore the internal chatter that feeds it. All day every day my subminds spam my consciousness with noise, and when I meditate I repeatedly ignore them. If I do this often enough—it has to be every day; it doesn't seem to work if it isn't—I create a high-level prior of my own: that their endless chatter is not important. My brain doesn't fill with noise, and the subminds stop waking me at 1am.

I try to meditate for half an hour first thing in the morning, another half an hour in the evening. The morning session seems to be the most effective. But there's a tension between my desire to meditate because it's important for my mental health and my desire not to because it's dull. Over the weeks and months, my practice follows a sawtooth pattern. I'm enthusiastic and diligent for a while, but it's nice to sleep in on weekends. Then I drop the weeknight evening sessions. I skip a couple of weekly morning sessions. My equilibrium starts to slip, usually so slowly that I don't notice it until I start waking in the night. There are other subtle and not so subtle signs, like indecision, mood swings, feelings of blind rage if the automatic doors at the supermarket don't detect my presence. Because I know these are warnings, I rededicate myself to the practice.

There's a pleasant clarity to the mind when I'm in one of these dedicated phases. If you think of your subminds as guests at a dinner party, the ones who shout the loudest are the most annoying. If you can get them to calm down you'll hear from the quieter guests, who tend to have more interesting thoughts. When I'm in this space I also experience moments of no-thought, when I notice something trivial but beautiful in the everyday: most recently the pale green mould growing inside my porch light, revealed when I switch it on at night, and I stop and look at it, and think about nothing.

But it is not a panacea. I can't meditate my way out of serious depressive episodes. I doubt many other people can either. 'Try meditation' is probably not useful advice for people who are very sick, and it might not be useful advice for a lot of people who suffer from anxiety and depression. The brain is complex. Mood disorders are complex. They're probably multiple conditions with different pathologies that have been grouped together because the symptoms are similar. But I believe that there's a subset of people like me, whose problems involve information and distraction and uncertainty, and that mindfulness is an effective long-term way to manage our illness. And I find the predictive processing framework useful because it makes sense, at least to me. Which is important, because it's hard to maintain a daily habit that feels nonsensical even if it works.

It might all be wrong. Psychiatrists and neurologists always think they're on the verge of understanding the mind and its disorders. They've thought this for over a century and all the theories have been wrong. But if our minds are computational, it seems inevitable that some of their problems will be computational: broken loops, intractability, complexity. Noise in the data.

So what are the jhana states? Nobody knows. The meditation author and teacher Leigh Brasington theorises that the first jhana has something to do with distraction. For the purposes of day-to-day survival you don't want your brain to have reactions to its own reactions. You don't want to feel pleasure in response to pleasure, and you really don't want pain in response to pain. So both qualia fade over time. The mind switches its attention to something else.

Economists sometimes talk about 'Knightian uncertainty': uncertainty about uncertainty. This is when you don't know things about the world, but you don't know what you don't know, and if you're an animal like the weka or a pre-modern human, not knowing things can kill you. Rapidly cycling between subminds is an attempt to minimise this risk. But you can circumvent this cycling by taking various recreational drugs that flood the pleasure circuits of your brain with neurotransmitters, or you can use concentration meditation to stay on the sensation of pleasure and allow it to amplify itself, which is how the first jhana seems to work. And this feels very nice. I mean, it is literally bliss. But bliss is less interesting than you think.

If we go back to the Buddha sitting beneath a tree and achieving awakening, whatever that is, the Pāli scriptures teach that he did this first by mastering the jhanas, then by practising a different form of meditation—vipassanā, or insight meditation. This is the technique that allegedly reveals the true nature of reality.

Some people who meditate a lot claim they've seen past lives or guardian angels, other planes of existence, and I don't believe any of them. But I have met dedicated meditators who've seen . . . something. They find it hard to describe. Non-existence. Cessation. Emptiness. They say it's an experience rather than an idea. Whatever they see, it transforms the way they experience reality and this transformation seems to be measurable. All around the world, neuroscientists are stuffing Buddhist monks with hardcore meditation practices into fMRI and PET scanners and finding that their brains look and function differently from everyone else's. They're subjecting them to psychological tests and finding that insight meditation makes them calmer and happier than the rest of us.

Concentration meditation is about training your brain to concentrate deeply. Insight meditation is about what you do with that concentration. There are different techniques. Maybe you note every thought or sensation that passes through your mind; maybe you focus intently on the individual components of the breath; or you turn your attention to your body and scan different parts of it to feel, say, your blood pumping through your circulatory system or even just the routine traffic in your peripheral nervous system that your mind normally filters out.

When I sit in access concentration for long enough—and the final day of my retreat in Wangapeka, the day after the jhana, is almost the only time I've been able to do this—and practise vipassanā techniques, a number of interesting things happen. The first is that I stop thinking in terms of language. I no longer have access to the idea of an inhalation or exhalation, or a nose or an abdomen, or even a breath. That submind no longer projects its thoughts into consciousness. Instead, I experience the sensations of the breath in ways that are a little hard to describe, because the whole experience is wordless, but 'wavelike' comes pretty close.

And it's an unstable state. It's easy to spill out and think in words again. Eventually it stabilises and I notice there's a granular quality to my thoughts. Our consciousness seems like an unbroken stream, but during insight meditation it presents itself as a sequence of discrete constructs. Once I observe this I notice the gaps between the thoughts, which we've trained ourselves not to notice, like the spaces between words in a sentence. These start out as brief flickers of nothing, but as my thinking simultaneously slows down and speeds up the individual sensations become slower and slower, until I see each separate thought bubble up, out of nothingness, and then evaporate. This is an awe-inspiring experience. When I think about it afterwards, it feels like I've witnessed the heart of the hard problem: the alchemical moment when the electrochemical signals in the brain transform themselves into conscious thought.

People who dedicate years to this type of meditation have insight experiences. They don't see past lives or heaven. They see—so they say—glimpses of reality, the true nature of mind, the emptiness of material existence. The cumulation of these moments leads to awakening.

I haven't had many insight experiences. I don't have time. I have a family, a job, a mental health problem to deal with. Stuff on TV I want to watch. I feel very far from awakened. But I see what they're saying about emptiness. There is a powerful sense of nullity when I glimpse these moments between thoughts—a sense of annihilation. When I recall it, I think about Heidegger's premonition of the nothing that lies beyond the visible world. I wonder if depression and anxiety are just biological malfunctions, closed loops, or whether there are alternate ways of seeing and being in the world, which mood disorders point us towards. I think about the time I hid my daughter's toy and made her cry, and the idea that high-level abstract priors embedded deep in our minds, existing beyond language or rationality—priors like object permanence—lock us into fixed perceptions of reality. I wonder if the insight meditators are updating those priors, if they're perceiving existence in ways the rest of us cannot.

And I think about trails through the trees, leading to on-ramps and expressways, down unlit halls, footprints on the beach, neurons opening into synaptic clefts, paths through the dunes, recondite pathways forking and branching. I wonder if they all lead back to themselves, a series of interconnecting labyrinths with no exits and no centre, or whether there really is a way through the maze, a clearing in the mind where the world opens up to itself. Some vast neurochemical valley, flooded with probability and light. A place and a state outside the hallucination.

The Child and the Open Sea

I am one of the first to arrive. The organisers are setting up, arranging trestle tables and chairs into a horseshoe formation in the main hall. This is a large room with a whiteboard along the front wall. At the back is a door leading to a separate kitchen stocked with enough food to last thirty people for four days. Few of these people know each other, so Catherine—the main organiser, who makes self-effacing comments about how everything runs itself while being very obviously the person who runs everything—writes a list of icebreaker questions on the whiteboard. When the guests arrive they can pair up and discuss them. The questions are:

- Is the world going to continue to get better in the next twenty years?
- Should we take wild animal suffering seriously?
- Assuming we can impact them, does someone born in one thousand years' time matter as much as someone alive today?
- Is 100% of people dying much worse than 99% of

people dying?

- Is artificial intelligence an existential risk to the future of humanity?

When she's finished, she shows me to my room, which is in an accommodation unit further down the long gravel driveway.
The campground is in a remote valley east of Wellington. The site is owned and operated by the Boys' Brigade Charitable Trust. Everything is well made but extremely utilitarian, designed to withstand prolonged exposure to hordes of barely supervised small boys. The sleeping quarters are dorm rooms: mine is small and square with a woodchip floor, four bunk beds, a metal chair, and a bare, bright lightbulb in the ceiling. The walls are painted not-quite-green. I set up my sleeping bag then return to the main building.

The organisers are eating lunch at the picnic tables beside the main hall. It's the middle of winter but sunny and warm. The camp is encircled by hills covered in native bush; they look like green sine waves. The sky is unrealistically blue. 'It all looks photoshopped,' Catherine announces. She's in her mid-thirties, vegan-lean, like everyone who attends this retreat except for me. She's a former physicist, but when I ask her about her PhD she rolls her eyes. 'It was on the mathematics of neutrino particles and their implication in grand unified theories,' she tells me. 'I used to want to know the deep secrets of the universe but now I don't care about that at all.' Instead she cares about effective altruism. She wears a T-shirt with the logo of the effective altruist movement: a drawing of a lightbulb with the filament fashioned into the shape of a heart.

*

In 1972 the philosopher Peter Singer published an essay called 'Famine, Affluence and Morality'. It invited us to imagine ourselves in a deceptively simple scenario: you're walking along the road, wearing clean clothes, when you come across a child you've never seen before drowning in a shallow pond. Do you wade in and save the child? And of course you do. Or, at least, you say you do but, Singer argues, you don't. About 17,000 children in the developing world die from starvation or treatable diseases every day, as of 2018—while the residents of the developed world spend most of our money on nonessential luxuries. It shouldn't matter, Singer argues, that the children die in another country instead of directly in front of us. The moral obligation to help them is the same. Especially if that help comes at a very low cost to us.

It's hard to reject Singer's logic, but if you accept it then you're confronted with challenging questions about the morality of your daily life. If I buy a doughnut at the mall, that money could have gone to bed nets coated with an anti-malarial compound or schistosomiasis treatments in the developing world, so buying a doughnut means letting a child die. And the needs of the world are so vast that anything I spend beyond what I require for my basic survival cannot be justified. Every doughnut I eat points to terrible suffering.

Some people read Singer's essay and change their lives. They retrain as doctors and work in the developing world or live very frugally in their own country and donate the bulk of their money to charity. But when I first read the essay, sometime in my early twenties, my reaction was one of cognitive dissonance. I liked to think of myself as a good person, but I also liked doughnuts and other nice things, and if I thought about the money I squandered it was increasingly obvious that I wasn't a good person at all, so I tried not to think about the drowning child and I kept spending money on myself.

But sometimes—and it is often at the mall—I glimpse myself in some reflective surface: a middle-aged man with caramel glaze in his beard, the lenses of his glasses blank with reflected light, and I suddenly feel very selfish. In these brief moments, my life, which is mostly a pleasant and contented thing, seems frighteningly trivial.

I sit at the picnic table and introduce myself to Sophia, who lives in Sydney. She studies mathematics and economics. She's here because she's the community manager for Effective Altruism Australia and New Zealand. This will be the second retreat for the New Zealand branch of the movement. Last year, fifteen people came. This year, it's just over thirty. Which is a lot, and Catherine and Sophia look at the questions on the whiteboard and wonder whether they need a Python script to algorithmically sort people into groups with maximally diverse opinions. Or should they start with an icebreaker game? But once people arrive, it is clear that no icebreakers or sorting algorithms are required. Newcomers drive up, find a room, insert themselves into groups in the main hall, and start talking and do not stop for four days. Most of them are in their twenties or thirties. Almost all of them have studied some combination of maths, economics, philosophy and computer science. Many of them are here because at some time in their late teens or early twenties they googled 'How can I make the world a better place?' and found their way to an effective altruist website, podcast, or YouTube clip.

I introduce myself to K, who studied philosophy and maths, did honours-level philosophy, spent a year travelling around Africa, and is now training to be a maths teacher.

'What areas of philosophy did you specialise in?' asks

someone in our group who is also a mathematician and philosopher.

K replies, 'Aesthetics and anti-natalism.'

'That's a weird combination,' the first philosopher observes. K does not respond.

I ask him, 'Are you . . . an anti-natalist?' I have never asked anyone this before, and I feel immediately awkward. It is a strange thing to ask a person whether they think that none of us should have been born. But K is not a guy who seems highly attuned to social awkwardness. He's an intense figure with buzz-cut hair and angular cheekbones.

'I am,' he replies. 'I'm an adoptionist. I think that birth has negative value. You shouldn't bring new life into the world, partly because existence is suffering, but also because there's pre-existing life we should care for.'

'What are the good texts on anti-natalism?' the other philosopher asks.

'*Every Cradle is a Grave*,' K replies quickly. 'It's excellent. It's tough to be an anti-natalist though. We don't breed, so we're dying out. And everyone thinks we're weird. Even the effective altruists think we're weird, and they're already pretty weird.'

*

It took a long time for the ideas in Singer's drowning child essay to cohere into a movement.

In 2007, a pair of New York-based hedge fund analysts called Holden Karnofsky and Elie Hassenfeld decided to donate some of their rapidly increasing fortunes to charity. Hedge funds try to maximise the value of their clients' investments by researching and estimating the future value of different companies, then investing in the most profitable predicted ventures. So Karnofsky and Hassenfeld decided to do the same with their charitable donations. They knew that running profitable companies was hard: people did dumb things, lost money and went bankrupt, while other companies succeeded and flourished. Surely it would be the same with charities? And, since your donation was intended to save lives and end suffering, surely it was even more important to make careful, considered choices about where the money went?

They began calling charities and asking to see their data. What were they doing? How did they know their methods worked? How many people did they help last year? How many did they intend to help next year? What were their metrics? But very few charities had any quantifiable data or anything that could be used to measure the efficacy of their work, let alone to compare them with other charities.

Karnofsky and Hassenfeld knew that companies that operated like this went bankrupt very quickly, but this didn't seem to happen if you were a charity, especially if you had good marketing. People just kept on giving you money. Many of these organisations operated in complex, chaotic environments—failed states, warzones, regions devastated by drought or disease—but the people running them were often well-meaning westerners who didn't seem to know much about these places.

What you needed, Karnofsky and Hassenfeld decided, was a charitable version of a hedge fund: a meta-charity that gave money to other charities based on the measurable impact of their work. They quit their day jobs and founded GiveWell, an NGO devoted to this task, and quickly determined that charitable work was even more divergent than financial investment. Some charities did enormous good while many seemed to accomplish little, or nothing other than provide salaries for the executives who ran them and the marketing experts who promoted them. And some charities failed at what they did so spectacularly that they were actively making things worse for the people they were trying to help.

By 3pm most of the group has arrived at the campground. About thirty people are assembled in the main hall. Catherine calls for silence, then Sophia addresses the crowd. She congratulates the New Zealand Effective Altruists on successfully establishing the movement here. 'According to the 2018 global EA survey, New Zealand has the highest number of effective altruists per capita in the world!'

There is a brief burst of chatter from all the economists and mathematicians in the room as these results are parsed for statistical significance. It does not sound likely: there are five million people in New Zealand, and many of the effective altruists in the country are in this very room. Maybe there is a selection bias in the survey responses? An error in the population data? Obviously, more research is needed.

Catherine shuts them up, then Sophia continues. 'Building this community is so important,' she tells the room. 'It's hard when you have values that are so different from those of the people around you. Especially if you're working in finance or tech, and you're tithing and everyone around you has so much while you have so little. So just being here for each other can be everything.'

Some of the people around me agree with this sentiment. It is hard being vegan and tithing to a meta-charity and believing in various widely-regarded-as-weird things which I will describe presently. But others are more stoic. They know they are weird and don't especially care, and they go back to arguing about anti-natalism until Catherine interrupts again to point out that it's a beautiful day and that the camp is surrounded by walking tracks through lush native bush, and sends everyone outside.

The poster child for catastrophic charitable failure is the Roundabout PlayPump. Everyone in the EA movement knows about PlayPumps. They were invented by a South African engineer called Ronnie Stuiver. He noticed that women in poor rural villages across Africa spent a lot of time pumping water, while kids in wealthier suburbs spent a lot of time at their local parks playing on merry-go-rounds. What if you combined the two and built a merry-go-round attached to a hydraulic system in the village well? Kids in poor villages would have something to play on, and the women wouldn't have to pump water all day. You could sell advertising on them, and this would provide a revenue stream for maintenance. The whole idea was simple and magical and perfect: a marketing department's dream. The PlayPump was endorsed by Laura Bush, Bill Clinton, Beyoncé, Jay-Z. It attracted tens of millions of dollars in funding. Thousands of PlayPumps were installed across the poorest, most impoverished regions of Mozambique.

Which was a shame, because the PlayPump turned out to be a truly terrible idea. Children play on merry-go-rounds because they're easy to spin around, but PlayPumps were hard to spin, because they were . . . water pumps. And water is heavy. So children didn't play on them. The women in the villages still had to pump water, but pumping water using the PlayPump was much harder than using a regular pump. It was, the women in the villages complained, a humiliating device for grown-ups to operate. The pumps broke down all the time. They were expensive to fix. No one wanted to purchase advertising space on them, because they were deployed to some of the poorest people in the entire world, so there was no money to fix them.

GiveWell's goal was to support charitable aid that was cheap, effective and measurable—the opposite of the PlayPump. They discovered a handful of charities who were distributing anti-malarial bed nets, deworming children and giving them vitamin supplements. Projects that were not adorable or fun, but which did save or improve vast numbers of lives. There's an axiom in effective altruist circles that if a cause or charitable organisation is simultaneously helping those in need and validating the emotional needs of the donors, it's probably only doing one of those things well, and it's probably the latter.

In 2009 the Oxford philosophers Toby Ord and William MacAskill founded Giving What We Can. They'd read Peter Singer's work and decided to form an organisation based on his moral principles. People who joined Giving What We Can committed to donating at least 10 per cent of their income towards effective charity for the rest of their lives.

Ord's research led him to the same conclusions as the GiveWell founders across the Atlantic: some charities were far more effective than others. But the difference wasn't simply the competence of the organisations; it was *where* the charities operated. He cited donations to the blind: you could donate to organisations in the developed world that trained guide dogs, which at the time cost approximately US$40,000 per dog, or you could donate to an organisation in the developing world that prevented people from losing their eyesight due to trachoma infection. Each trachoma treatment cost $25. Donating to the trachoma charity was 1800 times more effective than donating to the guide dog charity.

In 2011 MacAskill and Ord founded another organisation, 80,000 Hours, which is designed to give free career advice to people looking to accomplish the greatest possible amount of good during their lives. (Eighty thousand hours is the estimated amount of time you'll spend working throughout your career. EAs call the organisation '80k'.) In 2012 they started the Centre for Effective Altruism, an umbrella non-profit designed to coordinate the overall movement, which had already spread to London, Europe and the US, advancing at a faster rate than anyone could have expected for a philosophical movement based on charitable tithing and statistical rigour. In 2015 MacAskill published *Doing Good Better*, which set out the principles of effective altruism:

> Effective altruism is about asking 'How can I make the biggest difference I can?' and using evidence and careful reasoning to try to find an answer. It takes a scientific approach to doing good. Just as science consists of the honest and impartial attempt to work out what's true, and a commitment to believe the truth whatever that turns out to be. As the phrase suggests, effective altruism consists of the honest and impartial attempt to work out what's best for the world, and a commitment to do what's best, whatever that turns out to be.

*

A surprising number of trails at the children's camp lead to sudden plunges down deep gullies, or gloomy clearings with abandoned cabins, or swiftly flowing streams. We follow them all, trying to map optimal paths through the terrain.

I find myself next to Sophia again, and ask her about her cause area. Most EAs have a single issue that they're especially interested in. Global poverty and animal welfare used to be the big ones, but as the movement has grown and diversified so has the number of causes. She tells me she's drawn to global priorities research. This is meta-research—the researching of research. For instance, some effective altruists believe that science is not very scientific. Every year the world spends at least half a trillion dollars on research, but there are no coordinating principles to determine what kind of research gets done. Same idea here as with the meta-charities. Some forms of research are more impactful than others. If you research research, then the world can reprioritise that $500 billion per year to the most impactful research and deliver better outcomes for everyone.

The group ahead of us is talking about books. K the anti-natalist is reading *Infinite Jest* and *Wuthering Heights*. '*Infinite Jest* is good,' he explains. 'It's about hedonic consumption. Metaphysics. Nuclear war. I get all that. But *Wuthering Heights* is terrible. She's in love with some guy. Who cares? I don't get it.' As the trail narrows and we draw nearer, he turns and demands to know what we've been reading.

Sophia's been reading Ursula Le Guin's Hainish books—everyone murmurs approvingly—and macroeconomics texts. I've been reading *Reasons and Persons* by Derek Parfit, and this is a very acceptable response. *Reasons and Persons* is better than *Wuthering Heights*, maybe even better than macroeconomics.

If Peter Singer is the atheist prophet of effective altruism, Derek Parfit is the rational messiah. An Oxford philosopher, Parfit is less well known than Singer, but in academic circles his work is more influential. When he died in 2017, he was eulogised as the most important moral philosopher of the twentieth and early twenty-first centuries.

'How long did it take you to read that?' K asks.

'About four months.'

'Really? It took me six months.'

'Maybe I didn't understand a lot of it,' I suggest. K nods, accepting this as a very credible explanation.

Reasons and Persons is difficult. Especially if, like me, you don't have a background in academic philosophy. Parfit spent most of his life working and residing at All Souls, Oxford. Some of his obituaries mentioned that it was rare for him to encounter non-philosophers in his day-to-day life. His book assumes a reader who will grasp the deep implications of everything he's saying, because he certainly doesn't feel the need to spell it out. Important insights appear as cryptic asides or casual hints. At one point he remarks that his findings should not be communicated to the wider public and seems certain that the reader will honour this pact of secrecy. But I don't think you can understand the effective altruists without understanding Parfit.

There are two questions we can ask about the drowning child in Singer's pond, questions which would not occur to non-philosophers, but which lead down some interesting paths. Firstly, why do we feel an intuitive obligation to help the child? Where does that impulse come from? And secondly, is it rational to save the child?

Parfit would answer the first question by stating that we want to save the child because of 'common-sense morality'. This is a set of evolved intuitions about how we should behave towards each other. Natural selection has designed us to save children if they are dying directly in front of us. Biologists going back to Darwin have wondered how humans and other animals evolved a sense of morality. Where did values like altruism come from? If an organism in a species sacrifices itself for the greater good because it has a genetic disposition to do so, don't those genes get wiped out and replaced by nonaltruistic genes? Evolution is supposed to be ruthless, so why do we feel such a strong instinct to help one another?

Parfit argues that altruism and other values of common-sense morality are solutions to the routine problems of cooperation and reciprocation that arise between members of a social species. You might not be directly related to the child in the pond, but they're right in front of you, so your brain assumes they're a member of your community. One day another child that you are related to might be drowning in a pond somewhere else, and if you don't save this child then other members of your community might not save yours.

Parfit demonstrates this argument by invoking the prisoner's dilemma. This is a famous two-person scenario central to game theory. It was invented by a pair of RAND Corporation mathematicians in 1950, but remained somewhat obscure until the sixties, when biologists and social scientists figured out that the dilemma wasn't just a game: it was a metaphor for countless life-and-death situations involving risk, cooperation, uncertainty and trust.

You probably know it already, but if you don't it goes like this. You're a member of a criminal organisation. You and an associate are taken prisoner. The police can send both of you to prison for one year, or you can inform on your associate, in which case you'll go free and he'll go to prison for three years. If you both inform, you'll both go to prison for two years.

The best outcome *collectively* is for you both to remain silent. You'll both go to prison for one year. This is known as 'cooperation'. But cooperation requires an extremely high level of trust. If you think your associate trusts you and will cooperate, then your rational strategy is to defect, because then you will go free. And they'll think exactly the same thing about you. So if you have any uncertainty about your associate's choice—and you always do—then you'll both defect, and you'll both go to prison for two years. On an individual basis you can rank the outcome of prisoner's dilemma games like this.

Best outcome: You defect against an associate who co-operates. You go free.

Second best: You both cooperate. Both in prison for one year.

Third best: You both defect. Both in prison for two years.

Worst: You cooperate and your associate defects. You go to prison for three years.

Economists have conducted countless experimental studies of the prisoner's dilemma, matching different players against each other game after game. Most people start out cooperating, because we're a cooperative species. Cooperation is what common-sense morality tells us to do. But once they figure out the relentless logic of the game, subjects quickly switch to defection, because that's the self-interested rational solution, and then the other participant in the dilemma does the same, and everyone keeps defecting with each new opponent in each new game. By trying to win as individuals, everyone loses.

Game theorists call this a Nash equilibrium. It's the rational strategy you adopt when all other participants in a game adopt a rational strategy (and they adopt the rational strategy because they know you will too). And this is a really important point. In many games, and many real-life strategic scenarios, rational self-interest is the smartest thing to do, but it leads to a terrible outcome for everyone.

But there's another form of the prisoner's dilemma: the iterated prisoner's dilemma. This is where you play the same game against the same person, over and over. If someone defects against you in the first round, you can retaliate in the second round. The most rational strategy in the iterated prisoner's dilemma is called Tit for Tat: you cooperate in the first round, and then do whatever your associate does in response. Experiments show that these games almost always fall into a repeated pattern—or Nash equilibrium—of cooperate–cooperate. This gets both of you the second-best outcome as individuals, which is the best outcome for the overall group. So altruistic cooperation is better than—*more rational than*—rational self-interest.

And this is all a metaphor. Common-sense morality predates our species, and it worked beautifully in the small, relatively egalitarian communities we evolved in: bands of hunter–gatherers, villages, fishing and farming communities. These were the societies almost every single human ever born lived and died in, right up to the end of the nineteenth century. If you spent your whole life among a small group of people, mostly relatives, all of whom you knew and who knew you, and you then defected in a multi-player dilemma by stealing everyone's food, or sleeping when they were working, then everyone knew you were an untrustworthy sneak, and they'd fail to cooperate with you, which usually meant throwing you out of the village or tribe, at which point you'd die pretty quickly. So it was in everyone's interest to cooperate, or at least be seen to cooperate. But that moral framework breaks down once people start living in large, complex societies. Like nations or city states.

After the walk we return to the hall and play a game where we try to learn everyone's name. We stand in a circle and memorise the names of the people either side of us. If one of their names is called out but you fail to remember it, you're out of the game. It's a game that openly discriminates against slow-witted people with bad memories, and I am one of the first out. We play twice and a different mathematician wins each time.

Afterwards, Catherine breaks us into groups and tells us to discuss what we can offer the cause of effective altruism. 'The purpose of this retreat,' she reminds us, 'is that you want to dedicate your life to helping others, and you're here to figure out the best way to do that.' But my group just talks about how they all discovered effective altruism. For most of them it was at university, as undergraduates, and they're still part of a campus group and go to meetings. But some of the people on the retreat live in provincial towns where, they complain, there are no philosophers or mathematicians, let alone effective altruists. They came here on long bus trips overnight, because flying is too carbon-intensive, and the bus is cheaper, and they can pass on the saving to GiveWell. They can't quite believe they're actually here, surrounded by people who think like they do.

The *Republic*, a series of philosophical dialogues composed in Athens around 380 BCE, is ground zero for moral and political theory in the western tradition. Near the beginning of the work, Plato has Socrates ask a famous question: 'Why is it in one's interest to be just?' Why be a good person? Or, to reframe this in game-theoretic terms, why cooperate? Why not just go around the city lying and ripping everyone off? Remember, if you defect in a non-iterated prisoner's dilemma and your associates don't, you come out on top. You get released from prison, or you get to sleep while everyone else does all the work, or someone saves your drowning child but you refuse to save theirs. In a large, anonymous society like a city state, defecting is the individual's rational option. But if everyone does this and no one trusts each other, then nothing works and your society can't function. It can't feed itself, and it definitely can't defend itself from attacks by more coordinated societies.

Plato's solution to this problem is known as 'the noble lie'. The people of the City want to act in their own rational self-interest? Well, then, you simply invent a religion in which you tell everyone that the social order and everyone's place in it are the design of a supernatural being who will punish or reward them after they die. That way, it's in everyone's rational self-interest to cooperate with their fellow citizens, because cooperation is rewarded in the afterlife, while defection is punished.

Most modern commentators note that Plato has switched from asking 'Why is it in one's interest to be just?' to 'How can we manipulate everyone into being just?', but also that every complex society prior to the French Revolution was based on an organised religion that endorsed the moral authority of the state in exactly the way Plato described.

Most of these religions arose around the time of the *Republic*: Confucianism and Taoism in China, Judaism in the Levant, Jainism and Buddhism in India. This was a period of widespread urbanisation, when all of these societies encountered the problem of the non-iterated prisoner's dilemma. If we're to believe Plato—and many social scientists do—these religions were political solutions to the problems of coordination and trust. This is the point in history where common-sense morality becomes obsolete. It's now in your rational self-interest to cooperate, because God tells you to. Which is fine, so long as everyone believes it.

Plato's noble lie worked for about two thousand years, declining with the rise of scientific rationalism in the early modern period (philosophers regard the last five hundred years as 'modern'). Of course, many people in modern societies still have religious beliefs, but it's much harder for our leaders to tell us to behave ourselves because we'll be punished in our spiritual afterlives if we don't. We're taught to demand proof of such claims, and of course that proof can never exist. This is a problem, Derek Parfit tells us, because the moral theory of rational self-interest is hard-coded into our society and its institutions—our entire economy is based on it—but there's no longer any punishment for defection. And if everyone defects in any collaborative game the outcomes are bad. It's more rational to eat a doughnut than to save a dying child, if we assume they'd do the same to us.

*

Dinner on the first night is dhal with wholemeal rotis. The chef, an engineer with a PhD in mechanical electronics, asks for three volunteers to help him in the kitchen. Thirty people charge towards him, desperate to cooperate in the coordination game that is communal cooking. I happen to be standing near the kitchen door when this happens, so I'm tasked with rolling the roti breads.

While we cook we discuss existential risk, which is another term for the extinction of humanity, abbreviated as x-risk when you talk about it as often as the effective altruists do. 'If a nuclear exchange, pandemic, AI local explosion, meteor strike, super volcano, or extreme climate change event takes out most of global civilisation,' the physics student peeling potatoes argues, 'it might be a good idea to have vaults. These would be secure storage sites filled with plant seeds and data so that once civilisation emerges from the rubble it can jump-start several thousand years of scientific and technological development. Would New Zealand be a good site for such a vault?'

Concern about x-risk stems from another idea of Parfit's.

He invites us to compare three different future scenarios: no nuclear war, a nuclear war that destroys 99 per cent of the human race, or a nuclear war that destroys 100 per cent of the human race. Obviously, no war is better, but most people consider the second two options to be roughly comparable: 100 per cent of deaths is worse than 99 per cent, but 99 per cent is still really, really bad.

Parfit disagrees. The greatest difference between these two outcomes, he thinks, is between the second two scenarios. We shouldn't consider only the individual deaths caused by the catastrophe; we should also consider the lives that will not be lived if our species is destroyed. Our planet will probably be habitable for another billion years. The number of human lives that could be lived in the future is inconceivably greater than the number of people who have ever lived, or who are alive today (the number sixty-four quadrillion is often cited.)

Because of the vast number of actual and potential lives lost in an extinction event, the third option is an x-risk. It is 'uniquely bad'. Most of us fail to worry about x-risk because no such catastrophe has happened to our species before, by definition, but most effective altruists believe we have a very strong obligation to worry about x-risk because of the number of potential lives involved. If we have a duty to current populations living on the other side of the world, do we not also have a duty to future populations separated from us by time?

'We're unlikely to be targeted in a nuclear strike, but we're seismically unstable,' the woman chopping onions next to me points out, then asks, 'and how would you store the data?'

'You could do what the Scientologists have done with L. Ron Hubbard's texts,' I suggest. 'They're engraved on stainless steel tablets and encased in titanium capsules in the tunnels beneath a compound in New Mexico. Hubbard's texts are more likely to survive the extinction of our species than almost any other human artefact.'

That sounds like a good technique, the room agrees excitedly, but when we're eating dinner someone objects by raising a meta-point: Effective Altruism is already seen as rather strange. It wouldn't do to be caught imitating the Scientologists.

I wake early the next morning. I've chosen the dormitory furthest from the main hall, so I have this bunkroom to myself. I meditate for a few hours but it's still dark when I go outside. The hills around the campground rise up against the sky like probability curves; the stars above them are non-randomly distributed, clustering in a thick diagonal band across the southern quadrant of the night. There are no sounds except the white noise of the stream and the wind in the trees, and these are eerily loud amidst the general silence.

I'm the first person in the main building. The trestle tables are covered in laptops and power cables and cellphone chargers, the cables overlapping in complex topologies of arcs and curves. Someone has left a biography of the mathematician Srinivasa Ramanujan on the kitchen bench; someone else has drawn Sierpiński triangles all over the whiteboard in an attempt to explain the plot of *Infinite Jest*. Barely legible beneath the fractal geometry is a retreat schedule, which includes talks on rationality training, Africa, wild animal suffering, biosecurity, more rationality, feeding the world after a nuclear war, AI safety, and a session arguing against the principles of effective altruism, because the effective altruists are haunted by uncertainty and obsessed with asking themselves if they're getting everything wrong. Breakfast consists of Weetbix and almond milk.

One of the student leaders of the New Zealand EA movement

enters and absorbs the schedule. 'Two hours of rationality training? That's just crazy.' She makes a decaffeinated coffee, then sits at the trestle table at right angles to mine and begins making elaborate notes in a diary. 'I'm bullet journaling,' she explains. 'It's the optimal way of combining a diary, a to-do list and a planner. You should try it. It's easy once you've got your head around the symbolic alphabet and the indexing.'

'It all sounds awfully on-brand for EA,' I observe. The organisation is obsessed with optimisation.

'It is on-brand,' she admits, laughing and looking a little sheepish but then giving me a quick, sharp look and writing something in her journal: a series of symbols that I cannot decipher. The room fills up. People sit alongside strangers and spark up conversations. The first round of rationality training begins at nine thirty.

Rationalism is an intellectual movement that is separate from but overlaps heavily with effective altruism. They both emerged among philosophical and technological intellectuals in the early decades of the twenty-first century, dialoguing with each other, cross-pollinating. At its best, rationalism is a cross between philosophy of science, cognitive psychology and self-help. Rationalists study bias, judgement, probability, logic, uncertainty, all with the end goal of clarifying their thinking. At worst, the rationalists are exactly what you imagine about a group of people who call themselves 'the rationalists'. ('If we were as rational as we claim,' one treasonous rationalist confided to me, 'we'd call ourselves anything other than the rationalists.') There's an often-retold anecdote about a non-rationalist effective altruist being invited to a rationalist meet-up in the San Francisco Bay Area, the spiritual heartland of the movement, and asking what kind of people would be there.

'Oh, programmers,' they were told, 'and software engineers, computer scientists. All sorts of folks.'

'The Bay Area rationalist community has secret books,' another rationalist tells me—using her fingers and a tone of deep scorn to put quote marks around the words 'secret' and 'books'—'that they claim they can't release to the public because the techniques inside them are "too dangerous".' She rolls her eyes.

Rationalism is the belief that there is an objective, real world; that external reality exists; that humans can discover the truth about it and make logical decisions in order to influence future events, and that the scientific method is the best way to do this. But, somewhat paradoxically, many high-profile rationalists are interested in science fiction and science-fiction adjacent concepts like cryogenics, the Many-Worlds interpretation of quantum theory, the idea we're all living inside a computer simulation, the looming technological singularity—ideas that are considered somewhat fringe in mainstream scientific circles, but which many rationalists feel are rational. They believe in them, after all, and are they not the rationalists?

(The rationalists hate Spock from *Star Trek*, by the way. Eliezer Yudkowsky, one of the founders of rationalism, refers to Spock as 'the naive archetype of rationality', pointing out that Spock is always calm, even when calmness is wildly inappropriate, and he's always giving uncalibrated probabilistic estimates with many significant digits that are off by many orders of magnitude.)

The last two hundred years of western philosophy can be read as an ongoing and still unresolved conflict between the champions of scientific rationalism and their critics. (Nietzsche famously dismissed scientists as the priestly caste of modernity, and announced, 'There are no facts, only interpretations.' The linguist Steven Pinker, in his book *Enlightenment Now*—a defence of science and other enlightenment values—did not actually refute Nietzsche's arguments, which still prove frustratingly slippery, but he did encourage everyone to simply stop reading and teaching Nietzsche, while the Marxist theorists of the influential Frankfurt School attacked the Enlightenment as a failed project responsible for most of the problems of the world: 'The wholly enlightened Earth is radiant with disaster triumphant.')

Singer and the effective altruists remain unfashionably attached to rationality, as, obviously, do the rationalists. But in the second half of the twentieth century, science itself struck rationalism a terrible blow. A number of cognitive psychologists, most notably the Israeli academics Daniel Kahneman and Amos Tversky, convincingly demonstrated the non-rational basis of almost all human decision-making. Humans are capable of reason, Tversky and Kahneman's work showed, but the parts of our brains that we use for rational thought are recently evolved: they're slow, resource-hungry, inefficient, buggy. So when we make judgements, we prefer not to use reason. Instead, we use heuristics—mental shortcuts that let us make decisions quickly without resorting to rational analysis.

Here's a famous example: Linda is thirty-one years old, single, outspoken and very bright. She majored in philosophy. As a student, she was deeply concerned with issues of discrimination and social justice, and also participated in anti-nuclear demonstrations. Which is more probable?

- Linda is a bank teller.
- Linda is a bank teller and is active in the feminist movement.

Almost everyone picks option two, even though option

two is a subset of option one and cannot possibly be more probable. What's happening in the Linda Problem is known as the representativeness heuristic: we think that being a feminist is more representative of the description given to us of Linda than being a bank teller, and we base our decision on that instead of thinking clearly about the logic. The maths is correct but slightly challenging, so we ignore it in favour of a story, which is effortless but wrong.

In his book *Thinking Fast and Slow*, published a few years after he was awarded the Nobel Prize, Kahneman divided human cognition into two types: system one, which is intuitive and fast but which is highly prone to bias, and system two, which is attentioned and rational and logical, but also lazy and slow. Economists and other social scientists always knew that their models of humans as rational agents were flawed, but they also believed that markets would reward rational actors and thus incentivise more rationality. Kahneman and Tversky took great delight in proving that this was not so. They took the Linda Problem to statistics conferences and proved that the smartest statisticians in the world made the same blunders as everyone else. Heuristic bias and non-rationality are inescapable; they're hard-coded into human decision-making.

Many rationalists and effective altruists are haunted by this. They want to make rational decisions so they can make the world a better place, but their own brains are conspiring against them by making stupid, irrational system-one errors instead of sensible, logical system-two choices. 'There's even bias-bias,' one effective altruist whispered to me, her eyes wide with horror. 'It's when you think that because you're aware of cognitive bias, you think you're immune to cognitive bias, so you're biased about your exposure to bias.'

Another important influence on rationalist thought is a

political scientist called Philip E. Tetlock. Tetlock was one of the architects of the Good Judgment Project: a research programme that assembled large teams of experts with different backgrounds, beliefs, ideologies, political loyalties and skill sets, then challenged them to make specific predictions about future geopolitical trends. Will North Korea launch a new multi-stage missile? Will Greece remain a member of the EU? They scored the accuracy of the predictions and found that people with very strong political or ideological convictions did very poorly, often worse than if they'd guessed the outcomes randomly by throwing darts at a board. When you presented the experts with a relevant fact about a situation or choice, they accepted it if it supported their pre-existing model of the world and rejected it if it didn't. This didn't mean they were stupid; lots of them were highly intelligent. What it meant is that, when you're trying to think rationally, intelligence can be a problem as often as it's a solution. A high intelligence gives you a greater ability to explain away an inconvenient fact or justify an incorrect belief. If a subject is polarising—especially if it's closely linked to core forms of identity, such as politics or religion or ethnicity—then the smarter you are and the more you learn, the less accurate your understanding of that issue. And the more confident you become that your inaccurate understanding is correct.

But there's hope. A small number of forecasters in the Good Judgment Project were very, very good at making predictions: '30% better than intelligence officers with access to actual classified information'. Tetlock calls them 'superforecasters'. If you ask a normal person to predict the future—'Will there be a nuclear war in the next ten years?'—they'll make a judgement that's highly informed by cognitive bias. Maybe they don't like the current president of the US, or they recently read an article or saw a movie about nuclear war, so they decide that a war is pretty likely (the availability heuristic). Or maybe they've just had a child and their life is going well and they don't want there to be a war, so they judge it as unlikely (narrative bias). Rationalists want to be more like Tetlock's superforecasters, and make accurate, informed predictions about when we're all going to die. Rationality training teaches them how.

The effective altruist sitting next to me is in her late teens and is cheerfully eating a bowl of cooked white rice for breakfast. I point out the Weetbix and toast on the bench and she shakes her head.

'I can't eat any of that,' she replies. 'Not because I'm gluten intolerant or anything weird. I'm just a supertaster.'

'A supertaster?'

'Why does no one in effective altruism know about supertasting?' She looks annoyed for less than a second then happy again, like a fluorescent light flickering off and on. 'It's really common. The number of taste buds on your tongue'— she pokes out her tongue—'follows a normal distribution across the population and supertasters sit in the far tail of the curve. It's pretty simple.'

'It is simple,' I agree.

'Some biologists think we're an evolutionary strategy for detecting alkaloid toxicity in edible plants.'

I blink and point at her bowl. 'So to you, that white rice tastes . . . ?'

She hunches her shoulders with pleasure. 'So flavoursome. So good. I can't eat brown rice though. It's too intense.'

'So you can't eat, like, chocolate?'

'Oh my God, I love chocolate. Do you want some?' She produces a foil packet containing thin black squares, each about the size of a thumbnail. I hold one up and inspect it. There's an unearthly sheen to the chocolate, as if it doesn't reflect light the way ordinary matter does. 'This is pure processed cocoa bean with no milk or sugar,' she explains. 'Try it. It's incredible.'

I hesitate. I'm already addicted to chocolate, and I'm worried that if I try it in its pure form something terrible will happen to my life. But the supertaster is so good-natured it's impossible to say no. I put the tiny black square in my mouth and bite down.

'Isn't it amazing?'

The chocolate feels like a mass of wood pulp that's swollen to fill my entire oral cavity. I chew, slowly, and shift my tongue around, then shake my head. It's hard to talk, but eventually I swallow it back. 'That is the most weird, tasteless thing I have ever tasted. And that tastes good to you?'

'It does! It—' But then she shifts her attention. The rationality session is about to begin. 'Oh my God,' she breathes, her eyes glowing as the PowerPoint presentation shimmers into focus on the front wall. 'We're doing Fermi estimates!'

'The story goes like this.' The presenter is one of many tall, lean, bearded men with advanced degrees in computer science attending the retreat. He stands at the whiteboard, which he quickly covers with calculations. 'The physicist Enrico Fermi was one of the architects of the nuclear bomb. He was present at the Trinity test in New Mexico and wanted a rough estimate of the weapon's yield. So when it detonated, he tore up some strips of paper and as the shockwave from the blast reached his position at the observation post he scattered the papers in the air. He then estimated the mass of the paper, the distance the strips travelled, the distance from ground zero and the force required to shift the paper that distance and came up with an estimate that the destructive power of the bomb was equivalent to ten kilotons of TNT, which was astonishingly close to the actual number.

'The lesson,' the presenter explains, 'is when you're trying to figure out a probability or number, don't just guess. Break the problem down into separate components, get those components as accurate as possible, then add them all together.' Then he divides us into small groups and tells us to estimate the number of grains of sand in the world.

The effective altruists begin calculating. There's sand on beaches, obviously, and let's say beaches are 5 per cent of the world's coastline. Then you've got deserts. Tricky. The bottom of the sea. Very tricky. How deep is the sand down there? Does it go all the way down to the basalt, or is there a granite crust? How many grains are there in a cubic metre of sand? Too tough to calculate. How about a cubic millimetre? One hundred grains? Sounds about right. Now multiply it out. Everyone knows the diameter of the Earth is about 12,000 kilometres. Everyone knows that pi is exactly equal to three. Estimate that 10 per cent of the Earth is sand to a depth of one metre. Every group gets a different answer and the closest result is five times ten to the fifteen grains of sand, which is only a few orders of magnitude out from the answer on Wikipedia. Which was almost certainly reached by some form of Fermi estimate.

*

Derek Parfit suffered from terrible insomnia. He treated this condition with vodka and sleeping pills, which put him to sleep after about an hour but also gave him retrograde amnesia: he could never remember anything that happened during that final hour of waking.

One morning he found a letter on his bathroom cabinet. He'd written it during his window of amnesia, addressing it to his future self. His window-of-amnesia self had thought of something he wanted his future self to know about.

We should be rational, Parfit tells us, but we shouldn't be rationally self-interested, because rational self-interest is self-defeating. If everyone in a society follows rational self-interest you end up trapped in low-trust Nash equilibria in which everyone always defects, coordination problems cannot be solved and civilisation is impossible. The question is, how do you get people to put aside rational self-interest and be rationally altruistic instead?

Parfit's famously unorthodox solution begins with a discussion of split-brain syndrome. People who suffer from incurable epilepsy sometimes have the two hemispheres of their brain surgically separated. The divided hemispheres form separate personalities. In the most famous case, a split-brain patient whose left hemisphere wanted to get dressed would pull on his pants with one hand, but the other side of the brain, which did not want to get dressed, would yank them down with the other hand. One hemisphere would try to embrace his wife; the other would push her away.

The reason we act out of rational self-interest, Parfit argues, is that we believe in the existence of the self. We believe we are a person—that we each have an essential, indivisible quality inside us connecting our existence as a child with our lives today and our anticipated existence in the future. We make decisions in the interest of this future self, because we feel very strongly that this future person is us. But if we look at a person with split-brain syndrome, they seem to be two people occupying the same body. But no one has died. What has happened to that essential and indivisible self?

Parfit invites us to consider identical triplets who have all been horribly injured in a car crash. Two have had their brains destroyed but their bodies are fine, while the third has had their body destroyed while their brain is still intact. You could, hypothetically, take the intact brain from the third triplet, separate the hemispheres and place them in the two surviving bodies. Both would be a conscious person with the same memories as the other. This is theoretically possible, Parfit argues, citing the many stroke victims who have suffered extensive damage to a single hemisphere but have retained their identity, memories and desires, and still feel themselves to be the same continuous person.

What has happened to the unique individual self that occupied the brain and body of the third triplet before the hemispheres were separated? Parfit's answer is simple. Such a self never existed in the first place. He imagines the two bodies, each with a separate hemisphere. Once, when both hemispheres were in the same head, they thought of themselves as a single person, just as we all do. But now they are two people going off and living separate lives. Maybe one day they will meet again, play tennis and simply fail to recognise each other. This, Parfit argues, is how we should see our future selves. They are people whom we have some physical and psychological continuity with, but my future self is not 'me'— because there is no me. This is Parfit's solution to the problem of rational self-interest. We need to stop believing in the existence of the self. It's a once-useful fiction, like Plato's noble lie. In a much-quoted passage, Parfit wrote:

> Is the truth depressing? Some may find it so. But I find it liberating, and consoling. When I believed that my existence was a further fact, I seemed imprisoned in myself. My life seemed like a glass tunnel, through which I was moving faster every year, and at the end of which there was darkness. When

I changed my view, the walls of my glass tunnel disappeared. I now live in the open air. There is still a difference between my life and the lives of other people. But the difference is less. I am less concerned about the rest of my own life, and more concerned about the lives of others.

*

It wasn't until I reached my early forties that I figured out that being around large groups of people made me anxious. Before that, I thought of myself as individualistic. I didn't need other people, I could think for myself, and so on. Now I know that I need and like people and that I get confused if I try to think things through by myself, but I also know that too much time in crowds upsets me. And after the second rationality session I feel a little edgy, a little overwhelmed by all the social data washing around the room, so I go for a walk outside, following a gloomy wooded trail beside a stream.

This means I miss the 'What's Wrong with Effective Altruism?' session, in which the EAs critique their own belief system. This is part of the movement that's easy to mock, but the self-doubt embedded in the culture, the obsession with testing and measuring and questioning everything, is one of the things I think they get right. I've spent a lot of time on the fringes of progressive and environmental politics, and many of the marches and campaigns and causes I felt important, but I've often found myself asking the same questions about activism that the GiveWell founders asked about charity. What were we accomplishing? What were the goals? Where was the data?

My response to all these doubts was to become disillusioned and cynical, but the founders of effective altruism responded by founding effective altruism. Your intentions to be a good person and make the world a better place are admirable, it argues, but they aren't magical. Things won't get better just because you want them to. Real change is complicated. But you're a rich person living in a world of terrible suffering and you can make a difference.

I think about these things on my walk. The path along the stream is shadowy. Most of the trees have lost their leaves but the branches still push against each other, crowding out the sun. They look like elaborate data structures, bifurcating, cross-referencing, vying for maximal light.

When I get back, I ask the presenter of the Criticisms of EA session how it went. 'It was okay,' he reports. 'But I wish I could get some neo-Kantians in to really challenge us.'

'Utilitarians are always the bad guys in movies,' Sophia complains to me as we wash dishes together after lunch. The kitchen has a large window behind the sink, admitting the afternoon sun. From our position we look out over the campground. Small groups of effective altruists move purposefully about the muddy brown trails and bright green fields, dividing and converging like covariant data points on a vast dynamic scatterplot.

'Movie utilitarians consistently murder people for the greater good,' she continues. 'Haven't you noticed that?'

I explain that I have an eight-year-old child, which means I've only seen about eight non-children's movies in the last eight years, and ask, 'What movies have evil utilitarians?'

'There's *Star Trek* . . .'

'And Thanos in *The Avengers*.'

'He wants to solve the Malthusian trap by killing half the population of the universe,' one of the dish dryers scoffs. 'Why doesn't he just use the infinity gems to double the universe's available utility?'

'And don't these Hollywood scriptwriters know that many utilitarians are rule utilitarians?'

'What about Grindelwald in *Harry Potter*,' another dishwasher adds, and the entire room wails in despair. Most EAs are millennials and nerds; they love Harry Potter, so Grindelwald, who literally declares that his atrocities are 'for the greater good', feels like a particularly cruel betrayal.

Here is how the effective altruists like to think about morality. You have only one brief life. You want to use it to make the world a better place. But there are so many problems, so many different things that matter, so many careers you could choose and charities you could support and problems you could research. How do you decide? What is the right thing to do, and how do you know it's right? You take a utilitarian approach.

Utilitarianism is an ethical theory, a philosophical attempt to work out how we should behave, what types of behaviour our laws and institutions and culture should reward or punish. To many modern utilitarians, the most important fact about the universe is that it contains suffering. Because our actions can alter the amount of that suffering, we have a moral obligation to minimise it and increase happiness, thus bringing about 'the greatest happiness of the greatest number'. Which all sounds very rational but quickly leads you to a number of horrific moral quandaries. The most famous comes from Dostoevsky, who wrote in *The Brothers Karamazov*:

> Imagine that you are creating a fabric of human destiny with the object of making men happy in the end, giving them peace and rest at last. Imagine that you are doing this but that it is essential and inevitable to torture to death only

one tiny creature [. . .] in order to found that edifice on its unavenged tears. Would you consent to be the architect on those conditions?

Utilitarians reply that this seems like an unrealistic scenario, or that we should privilege the reduction of suffering over the promotion of happiness. But, like all good thought experiments, this can be translated into trickier scenarios. Should a police officer execute an innocent scapegoat to prevent a riot in which many will die? Should a surgeon sacrifice a healthy patient to save the lives of four dying people who need their organs? These are coordination problems, some utilitarians reply; people need to be able to trust their doctors and police, and if they defect against that trust it damages the overall good. But it is a tricky thing when you set out to maximise everyone's happiness.

Also, what is 'happiness'? Is it really the most important thing? If you had a choice between an immortal life as a barely sentient oyster who enjoyed a constant and unchanging low level of pleasure, or a much briefer human life filled with different intensities of both happiness and pain, few people would choose to be an oyster. Notions of happiness vary from person to person, and possibly species to species, so many utilitarians prefer the term 'utility', described in the nineteenth century by Jeremy Bentham, the philosopher most often associated with modern utilitarianism, as 'that property in any object, whereby it tends to produce benefit, advantage, pleasure, good, or happiness or to prevent the happening of mischief, pain, evil, or unhappiness'.

Almost anything that a conscious being wants is utility. But this question has been complicated further by Kahneman, who points out that there is a difference between pleasure and life satisfaction; most people rate the second as more important, but when given the choice we tend to prioritise the first. And people who chase after short-term happiness tend to rate their overall satisfaction as lower than average. If I want to eat a doughnut but I also want to be healthy and live a long life, which choice maximises my utility?

When effective altruist charities make decisions about what to fund and who to save, they often borrow a term from health economics, which is a deeply utilitarian field: the QALY, or Quality-Adjusted Life Year. If you spend a year in perfect health, that is worth one QALY. If you're blind or maimed, then a year of your life has a lower QALY score. If you want to figure out whether you should save two children from dying or cure ten middle-aged people from blindness, you add up the QALY scores and compare. If you're dead, you're worth zero QALY, and this is bad.

After lunch K talks to us about Africa. The continent is rapidly industrialising, he tells us, showing us slides of prosperous cities, wealthy suburbs. It's not the vast refugee camp some effective altruists think it is. But some of the traditional cultures are dying out. K was deeply moved by the traditional South Sudanese way of life. It's very religious and very altruistic and he wants effective altruists to reconsider their position that all human lives have equal value. 'Lives in weird cultures might have greater moral worth,' he argues, 'because they have so much to teach us, and when those lives are gone, the culture is gone.' Also, the Sudanese eat worms and, 'Worms taste amazing. They're the future of food. They are probably not sentient, although they do have rudimentary central nervous systems and we won't find out for sure until we solve the hard problem of consciousness. Technically they're caterpillars. And you can can them.' If teaching maths doesn't work out, K is thinking of importing worms into New Zealand. No one is ever quite sure when K is joking.

After the session, I ask him if there's a conflict between his anti-natalism and his belief that we should save the lives of people in weird cultures. 'Life shouldn't exist,' he explains to me. 'But realistically some lives will, so they should probably be weird lives with altruistic values. That's just pragmatic. And that's why Sudan is such a challenge to the assumptions of EA. If you have one culture that's deeply altruistic and another that practises modern-day slavery, do the lives in them really have equal value?'

The EAs are aware of the problems with utilitarianism and they discuss them endlessly. But most of them are still utilitarians, because it's the most rational moral philosophy. It's very easy to appeal to common-sense morality and say things like 'You cannot put a price on human life' or 'We should live in a world in which no child dies of hunger', which, sure, we should, but we don't. Instead we live in a world of suffering and limited resources, so if you say 'We can't put a price on the life of a child' and devote all of your resources to saving a single child, many more will die.

So when effective altruists examine a problem, they first look at the scale. How big is it? How many people does it impact? Second, how neglected is the problem? Lots of people around the world die of cancer and heart disease, but there are billions of dollars in research funding going into the prevention and treatment of these diseases. There's not much money going into distributing deworming pills or mosquito nets in the developing world, because the poorest people in the world don't vote or pay taxes in wealthy countries, so those political systems have no incentive to solve those problems. If you're a biologist thinking of going into cancer research and you decide not to, some other researcher will take your place and mostly do what you would have done. But if you research a developing-world disease, it's less likely that anyone else would be doing that work if you didn't. So this is a neglected problem, which means it has greater marginal utility, and you can make a greater difference if you focus on it.

The last piece of the EA formula is tractability. How solvable is a given problem? All of the highly rated GiveWell charities focus on healthcare and extreme poverty in the developing world, because these are solvable. If people living in rural villages in East Africa get sick because they can't afford roofs for their homes, you can just give them the money to buy a roof. Curing cancer, by contrast, is incredibly hard. Economists refer to this type of calculation as a utility function: you're ranking alternatives based on their utility to an individual or society.

But, some effective altruists wonder, why privilege human utility?

The next presentation is about animal suffering. About half of effective altruists don't eat meat, and most of them feel that modern factory farming is evil, one of the great horrors of human history. The food industry kills about sixty-five billion animals every year and most of them live lives of horrific suffering before they die. And none of it makes any economic sense. We have to produce the grains to feed the animals, but the animals squander most of that biochemical energy by shuffling around their pens and maintaining their internal body temperature. And consuming this meat is terrible for our health. And the animal's emissions contribute to climate change. All this suffering and waste, merely because many of us prefer foods with certain tastes and textures.

Today's presentation isn't about factory farming, though. It's about wild animal suffering. The number of animals in factory farms is large compared to the number of humans, but it's much smaller than the number of animals who live in the wild. There are at least one hundred billion wild land vertebrates and about ten trillion fish (Fermi estimates). Even if we count the moral worth and individual suffering of fish or insects as less than those of a human, the presenter of the next session argues that their sheer number makes any kind of human suffering trivial by comparison.

And living in the wild is horrible. We have an unrealistic, overly romantic view of nature, the presenter explains, shaped by wildlife documentaries and the marketing campaigns of mainstream conservation organisations. But almost all wild animal populations are caught in Malthusian traps: their numbers in any given ecosystem expand until they reach some natural limit, usually set by food availability, predators or disease, and then they crash again. Consider the snowshoe hare and the Canada lynx, a famous population pair occupying the boreal forests of North America. Snowshoe hares breed rapidly, and when their population grows the number of lynx who prey on them also increases. The hares live lives of sheer terror until they're eaten alive, and when most of them have been eaten, the majority of the lynx starve to death, at which point the hares repopulate and the cycle repeats. Or, consider the sea turtle. Its reproductive strategy is for the mother to give birth to about a thousand hatchlings, only one of which, on average, will survive to adulthood. The rest of them suffer agonising deaths, dying of dehydration or being torn apart by hungry birds. The scale of suffering of the sea turtle babies every hatching season is unimaginable.

So what are the solutions? How do we help the sea turtle

babies? Well, the presenter admits, there's a lot of research that needs to be done. Maybe we could use contraception to lower the reproductive rates of wild animals? Maybe use genetic engineering to stabilise populations? Predation is a hard problem, the presenter admits. It's difficult to maximise the utility of both the lynx and the hare at the same time. And ecological balance is paramount. Some wild animal suffering activists argue that the lives of wild animals are not worth living, that natural ecosystems are even more immoral than factory farms, but our presenter strongly disagrees with this. Instead he thinks there needs to be a new research field: welfare biology, a scientific field devoted to the study of the suffering of all sentient beings, and that the practice of conservation should be changed to a field of 'compassionate conservation', so that instead of just preserving animals, conservationists seek to minimise their suffering.

'But how solvable is any of this?' one of the biochemists in the audience demands. 'Humans are notoriously bad at designing large-scale complex systems. Look at communism. It keeps failing and that's only a political economy. You're talking about entire ecosystems here. This problem seems highly intractable.'

Other people want to know about the definition of a sentient being. 'There are new studies on insect sentience available on the EA website,' Catherine announces, and the session ends with an excited murmur as everyone opens their laptops and hurries to read them.

The second rationality session is about Bayesian reasoning and the importance of changing your mind. In 2015 Daniel Kahneman told a *Guardian* journalist that the most dangerous form of heuristic bias is overconfidence. Overconfidence causes:

the kind of optimism that leads governments to believe that wars are quickly winnable and capital projects will come in on budget despite statistics predicting exactly the opposite. It is the bias he says he would most like to eliminate if he had a magic wand. But it 'is built so deeply into the structure of the mind that you couldn't change it without changing many other things'.

Philip Tetlock's superforecasters are not overconfident. Instead they are highly uncertain. They change their minds as new data comes in, and when they're wrong about something they try to figure out why. What assumptions had they made about the world that turned out to be false?

One of the tools they use to do this is Bayes' theorem, a statistical model invented by an English Presbyterian Minister in the early eighteenth century. The presenter of this rationality session—a tall, bearded rationalist with black hair and unnervingly soft, liquid black eyes—uses the classic Bayes example taught to undergraduate statistics students the world over.

In this scenario your doctor wants to see if you have a rare form of cancer, one that afflicts one person in ten thousand. She gives you a clinical test with a 99 per cent accuracy rate and it comes back positive. What's the probability that you have the cancer? For most of us the answer—99 per cent—is obvious and of course it is wrong. A classic system-one error.

If the test is 99 per cent accurate, that means that for every hundred times the test is administered, one result is incorrect. Let us say it generates a false positive: it tells people they have cancer when they do not. But if the cancer has an incidence rate of one in ten thousand, then you have to give the test to ten thousand people before it correctly identifies a single cancer victim. If it's 99 per cent accurate, it will incorrectly identify one hundred people as having cancer when they don't, because even a 1 per cent failure rate adds up when you're working with large populations. If you plug these numbers into Bayes' formula it tells you the actual probability of you having cancer after taking the test, which turns out to be less than 1 per cent.

Here's why Bayes' theorem is important to the rationalists. The numbers you enter into the formula—the false positive rate, the actual cancer incidence—are known as your probabilistic priors. Because humans are irrational and the world is a complex place, your default priors about most important things are probably wrong. Is the test *really* 99 per cent accurate? Is the incidence rate of the cancer *really* one in ten thousand? A good rationalist will test those numbers and, if they're wrong, 'update their priors', which is statistical jargon for 'changing your mind'. Being wrong about things and changing your mind is a vital part of EA and rationalist culture. GiveWell and the other meta-charities are constantly carrying out Randomised Controlled Trials on their projects to try to figure out what they're wrong about, in an unceasing quest to check their priors and minimise uncertainty.

Dinner that night is spinach soup. I eat with the undergraduates, a cluster of young women from different universities who've met and bonded at the camp. They're studying a mixture of biology, maths, psychology and, inevitably, philosophy.

We talk about religion. Almost all of them grew up as Christians and lost their faith sometime in their teens. 'I was raised Catholic,' one explains, 'and I still have all this guilt and shame, and my response to that is to try and live a good life.' She shrugs. 'Guilt has utility.'

I'm excited to hear this. 'See, I have a theory,' I begin to explain, 'that EA is a post-religious—'

'A post-religious religion,' the ex-Catholic finishes. 'Yeah, a lot of people say that. Daniel'—she indicates with her head—'was at a conference last year where they talked about all the elements of organised religion that EA should adopt. All that community-building cultural technology.'

I must have looked deflated. 'It's hard to come up with new ideas about EA,' she says, sympathetically. 'A lot of smart people are interested in it.'

The conversation shifts to marriage. Weddings. Of course, they all agree, it's impossible to justify spending money on a lavish wedding ceremony when there's so much suffering in the world. But still, a wedding would be pretty great. And although EA used to be really frugal, they now say you shouldn't over-commit yourself to a life of austerity because that leads to burnout and is thus suboptimal. So maybe a moderately big wedding would be okay? They demand to know why I made the decision to get married. How did I know I'd found the right person? My answers are vague—'I just knew'—and obviously unsatisfactory. How did I gauge the uncertainty? What was my decision tree?

'I didn't have a decision tree.'

One of them makes a face. 'That's weird.'

'I don't . . . think it is.'

'I think boys are an optimisation and stopping problem,' another undergraduate announces. 'You just keep finding them and dumping them until you're thirty years old and then you keep the next one you like. That heuristic gets you the best candidate in the dataset about 37 per cent of the time no matter how large the search space.'

'But I'm really happy with the relationship I'm in now,' another undergraduate protests. 'And I'm only twenty.'

'Well, I'm twenty-one and I'm happy with my partner too,' the first admits. 'But can he beat the algorithm?' The conversation ends when someone calls for volunteers to wash the dishes and everyone in the room gets up and runs towards the kitchen.

The last session of the day is about AI risk. This is a divisive subject within the movement, and this is the only time I see any of the effective altruists get angry.

Media coverage of AI safety tends to focus on the *Terminator* movies, or video clips of terrifying robot dogs, or hypothetical scenarios in which a rogue AI turns the human race into paperclips. This is partly the fault of the rationalists, who are prone to elaborate futuristic scenarios featuring nanotechnology or galactic colonisation or other implausible claims about AI, which then get written up by journalists as 'Meet the nerds who think *Terminator* is real'.

To understand the actual AI problem, it helps to stop thinking about *Terminator* or *Blade Runner*, or any other movie, and start with the algorithms that run on Facebook's servers. These are known as a Narrow AI. They're not broadly intelligent. They're not robots. They're just code, and all they do is maximise the amount of advertising revenue the company's platform generates. They do this by trying to increase the amount of time Facebook users spend on the site and to increase their engagement with the advertising content, and they achieve this by endlessly analysing the metrics of Facebook's billions of users. Then they customise everyone's feed, using Bayesian updating to predict what people will watch, monitoring the outcomes, updating, predicting again.

During the middle years of the 2010s, the algorithm learned that most of us respond strongly to content that makes us angry or anxious or afraid. Consumers of the news stories or videos that provoked those emotions spent more time on the platform, they became more persuadable to the advertising, and they generated more content, which Facebook could then monetise with yet more advertising, and all of this was great for share value.

But once external organisations saw that this was the content the algorithm optimised, they started generating fake users, fake outlets and fake news deliberately calibrated to go viral on the platform, which was now the largest media outlet in the world by several orders of magnitude. And this had terrible real-world consequences, the two most well-known of which were the genocide in Myanmar and the interference in the 2016 US election by Russian Intelligence.

Facebook didn't want its AI to optimise for fake news, or anxiety or outrage, or to exterminate Muslim minorities in Myanmar, or to further Vladimir Putin's foreign policy goals. Its AI didn't know what any of those things were. All it knew is that it had a large database of users and a utility function to maximise their engagement and it had found the optimal way to do this.

AI researchers call this the alignment problem. How do you align the general goals that you give an algorithm, like 'increase engagement' or 'make money', with more specific goals, like 'Don't help the Myanmar military to kill people' and 'Don't help the Russians destabilise global democracy', goals that the designers weren't aware of until the AI breached them? AI research literature is filled with alignment problem failures, like a cleaning robot that was instructed 'Keep cleaning until you don't see any rubbish' and responded by switching off its cameras, or the algorithm programmed to win the highest score in a video game that simply rewrote the game code and assigned itself the top score.

The effective altruists are worried about Artificial General Intelligence (AGI). Facebook's algorithm was built to do one thing, but it could do it at superhuman speed and scale. In October 2017 the AI company DeepMind—a subsidiary of Google's umbrella company Alphabet—announced the successful development of AlphaZero, a machine-learning algorithm modelled on the pattern-recognition capabilities of the human brain. Within twenty-four hours of being activated, AlphaZero had achieved superhuman performance in chess, Japanese Chess and Go, a two-player game regarded by programmers as one of the most computationally intractable strategy games in the world. No one programmed AlphaZero to play or win at these games. They simply switched it on, told it the rules, then let it play against itself millions of times. A day later it could beat the most sophisticated pre-programmed AIs in the world at each game, all of which had been specifically designed to excel at them. And, obviously, all of those defeated AIs could easily beat the top-ranked human players.

What impressed other AI researchers about AlphaZero's performance was how creative the algorithm was. It didn't just use brute force to map out the consequences of moves in advance. (Solving a game like Go in this way is widely regarded as impossible; there are more potential moves in Go than electrons in the universe.) Instead it showed a deep and intuitive learned understanding of how to play.

AlphaZero is designed to win two-player perfect-information games—that is, games in which each player is fully informed of the other's previous moves, and nothing is hidden. It's not an AGI. But it's getting closer. A true AGI—which may still be decades away, but who knows—will be able to learn most or all cognitive tasks humans can do, and perform them on the same vast scale as existing algorithms, like Facebook's engagement software or Google's search indexer. That doesn't mean it will be conscious or that it'll suddenly turn on humanity and destroy us. Despite its wider capability, a general machine-learning intelligence will probably be just as unthinking as the code that runs on our phones.

This intelligence would not need to be programmed. An AGI deployed on a social media platform and told to maximise engagement could teach itself how to write video games, then generate highly addictive games; it could generate its own fake news stories; it could create plausible fake video footage on a massive scale, dwarfing the current production of all current media outlets combined; it could message people directly pretending to be human and it could do this with billions of people simultaneously. An AGI designed to execute trades on the global financial markets—and most of these transactions are already conducted by Narrow AIs—could invent new financial products. It could influence real-world events to maximise the value of a company or asset class. Or, like AlphaZero playing Go, it could do things that we simply cannot anticipate because it is operating at a superhuman level. Its human operators wouldn't understand why it was doing these things, and there's no guarantee they'd be able to switch it off. Maybe the AGI would try to maximise utility by rewriting its own code, or by creating a viral version of itself then infecting as many other systems as possible. Who knows?

Human rationality is bounded by biology and culture. An AGI would operate outside those constraints. But it would (probably) not be conscious, or sentient; it would just be trying to implement its utility function. And that's the danger. The Berkeley AI researcher Stuart Russell likes to compare an improperly aligned AGI to the legend of King Midas. When the king wished that everything he touched turned to gold, the god Dionysus didn't reply, 'Everything? Are you sure about that? Have you thought this through? Do you want your food to turn to gold? Your family? Everything?' The god does exactly what it's told, and the improperly aligned AGI will function the same way. AI risk advocates don't think we should worry about robots deliberately exterminating humanity. We should worry about a bank or a Silicon Valley tech company creating something incredibly dangerous because they think it might maximise shareholder value and blithely switching it on without considering the consequences.

This conception of AGI is controversial. Some AI advocates argue that any form of general intelligence will be, well, intelligent. It will have common sense. Its designers will be able to train it to be sensible and moral in the same way they train narrow AIs to play chess. But this is where the ideas of philosophers like Parfit intersect with arguments about machine learning. You don't want the AGI to have common-sense morality, because common sense is just a set of evolved intuitions that no longer function in complex societies, so it's *really* not going to function at the superhuman AI scale. To align an AGI with human values, you need a rational moral system that doesn't lead to horrific unintended outcomes.

'But how tractable is this problem?' K demands when the AI risk presentation summarising these arguments comes to an end. 'And how neglected is it really? Because it seems like anticipating and controlling the interests of a super-intelligent agent is the definition of intractable. Assuming this is a real problem—and I am not convinced it is—what's the solution? Global poverty is a problem. The solution is meta-charities. I get it. Animal suffering is a problem. The solution is to end factory farming. I get it. What's the solution here? You're going to do something to manage this risk, and it's something that the biggest companies and most powerful nation states with all the smartest people and experts in this area aren't doing and can't do, and that's why it's classed as neglected? And this thing will protect us from this hypothetical super-intelligent agent that will be able to outthink everyone in the whole world? Okay, but what is that thing? Why is this even a cause area? The uncertainty around all of this is incredible.'

There are murmurings of approval and nodding of heads from about half the people in the room, and I find that I'm one of the murmurers. K has articulated my own half-formed doubts about AI risk and voiced them in typically blunt terms.

There is uncertainty, the AI cause area advocates admit. High uncertainty. But because this is an x-risk threatening up to sixty-four quadrillion future lives, even a high level of uncertainty is wiped out by the scale of the problem. Most of the leaders of effective altruism have accepted the importance of AI risk. In a 2018 global survey of EAs, AI was ranked the second most important cause area after global poverty. Some organisations in the EA ecosystem are donating millions of dollars to machine-learning organisations and academic researchers hoping to solve the AI alignment problem. (GiveWell is not one of them: its focus is still global poverty, and its refusal to fund machine-learning research is a source of some bitterness from those effective altruists who believe AI risk is, logically, the single most important thing the movement can focus on.)

'Effective altruism used to be about global poverty and animal suffering,' one EAer complains to me after the AI risk session. 'And these are cause areas that lots of people care about and want to be a part of. It seems meaningful to them. But now you have all these people who are mostly rationalists, they're mostly computer scientists and software engineers, and they've constructed this ingenious argument for a cause area in which you invoke x-risk and save the world from this science-fiction trope through software engineering or by donating to computer science research, which happens to be the very thing they do for a living. And nice for them, if they actually believe this stuff. But to everyone outside the movement it just sounds bizarre. Foregrounding AI risk defines EA as a fringe movement that's basically only for tech people.'

I find this argument convincing, so I put it to one of the AI risk advocates, who is, as it happens, a software engineer. He's heard all this before.

'Imagine you're back in the 1930s,' he replies. 'And physicists start warning everyone that there's this new thing called nuclear fission and it could be really dangerous. It might lead to chemical reactions that could poison huge regions of the planet. You could build bombs with it that could destroy entire cities. They say we need to figure out how to manage this technology. Should people have said, "Bombs that could destroy a city? That just sounds bizarre. It's probably just physicists trying to inflate their own importance so let's not do anything about this." AI risk needs to exist as a field, the same way nuclear physics does, so we can study and manage its dangers.'

I find this argument convincing as well, and I spend the next hour moving between pro and anti AI risk advocates, being persuaded then counter-persuaded. People are still arguing when I get tired and leave, walking back to my dormitory in the rain.

*

The philosopher Kwame Anthony Appiah has a question for the effective altruists. You're walking along the road and you see the child drowning in its shallow pond. But this time you're wearing a very expensive suit. Do you save the child and ruin the suit, or do you let the child drown, right there in front of you, then sell your suit and give it to an effective altruist charity who can use the money to save two children?

No matter how committed you are to utilitarian logic, you're almost certain to save the child in front of you. So how viable is utilitarianism if almost everyone who believes in it defaults back to common-sense morality when challenged? If rational self-interest is self-defeating, as Parfit claimed, why not go back to common-sense morality and try to build institutions and an economic system that reflects our moral intuitions? We seem to be stuck with them anyway.

Parfit's answer to this is that, in a large complex society, common-sense morality is also self-defeating. To explain this he devises yet another thought experiment: the Harmless Torturers. Imagine a room filled with one thousand people strapped to instruments of torture. Besides each instrument stands a torturer. When the torturer turns the dial on their instrument the body of their victim is racked with pain. Common-sense morality tells us that the torturers are doing something wrong.

But now Parfit invites us to imagine a scenario in which each torturer turns a switch on their instrument that affects each victim's pain in a way that is imperceptible. Now the torturer can appeal to common-sense morality and argue that they're not doing anything wrong, that their actions as an individual have no perceptible consequences. But if there are a thousand torturers, each inflicting a tiny amount of pain, this adds up to the same agonising torture as the first scenario, but it's a form of torture no one person is directly responsible for.

Reasons and Persons was published in 1984, long before public awareness of climate change, but the Harmless Torturer is an almost perfect description of our moral attitudes towards carbon emission. Each of us sees ourselves as a Harmless Torturer: we go about our day-to-day lives in post-industrial society, each causing the trace emissions of tiny quantities of carbon, but all of this imperceptible activity aggregates into a vast, dire planetary catastrophe. And it is notoriously hard to convince people that this is a problem, because we don't have the moral concepts and language to think about collective responsibility, especially towards people who don't yet exist but who will face the consequences of our actions. Parfit believes we need a moral theory that solves the problem of the Harmless Torturer.

*

The third morning, it is still raining. It's much colder today, and as I get up, I hit my head on the top bunk. It really hurts. Outside the clouds are low, bleached out. It's cold.

'What about climate change?' someone asks over breakfast in the main hall. Most people are still in bed, but the rationalists who worry about AI are up, as are some of the AI risk critics, and they've resumed last night's debate. 'AI might be a potential risk,' a critic points out, 'but climate change is an actual catastrophe that's really happening.'

I've been thinking the same thing. There is an effective altruist climate charity called Cool Earth. It was co-founded by a Swedish billionaire and a British politician, and it's won various awards and commendations for being the most effective and impactful climate charity in the world. You give them money and they use it to buy tracts of endangered high-biodiversity rainforest, to prevent them from being chopped down. They place the land in trust to indigenous peoples of the area.

But it is fair to say that the wider movement is not focused on climate change. As of September 2020, GiveWell hasn't updated the climate change section of their website since May 2013. The 80,000 Hours website lists the two most neglected and important problems in the world as AI risk and pandemic risk reduction, while climate change is designated 'important but somewhat less neglected'. There's some debate among EAs about whether climate change qualifies as an x-risk, because some proportion of humans survive at almost any credible greenhouse gas concentration pathway. In the 2019 EA survey, when asked 'Which cause should be the top priority?', climate change was the second most popular choice, after global poverty.

'The problem of climate change is not neglected,' an AI risk critic points out as he walks around the room pouring out coffee from a plunger, 'but it's also not going that well. And almost every other cause area gets worse in a climate-changed world. Aren't nuclear wars more likely in a future with scarce resources and political instability? Isn't that an x-risk?'

There are more sessions, more presentations. The rain stops. People walk around the campground, planning future projects. There is a session on mindfulness in which the presenter asks, 'Does anyone here lie awake at night with your mind racing?' and almost every person in the room raises their hand. We hear about a scheme to feed the world in the event of a global catastrophe. 'You can extract a surprising amount of nutrients from leaf litter,' the presenter explains. 'The current population of the planet could survive on it during a nuclear winter.'

'So all we need to do to feed everyone,' one of the

undergraduates observes, 'is cause a nuclear winter and follow this plan.' Most people laugh but a few look thoughtful.

Dinner on the last night is pasta with tomato sauce and fried tofu. K is in charge of this meal. He gives me precise instructions on the dimensions of the tofu slices. It's hard to talk in the kitchen, because the conversation in the main hall is so loud. Even though they've spent the last four days together, in constant contact, the EAs are still talking to each other at high volume and high speed about poverty and machine-learning and the moral worth of animals and the threat of human extinction and all the other things they're obsessed with and can't understand why people outside the movement are so indifferent to. There are few obvious power dynamics in effect at the camp; there are no obvious cliques or status games. Everyone talks to everyone.

'My parents still donate to the SPCA, even though I've told them and told them that they use dairy in their cupcakes at fundraisers.'

'You should totally meditate. It attenuates the neurons in your amygdala and promotes cortical growth in your prefrontal cortex.'

'You've never heard of Hans Rosling? Oh my God, he practically invented data visualisation!'

After we serve the food, I load up my plate and find a place with a group of EAs I haven't talked to yet: a couple of programmers and a medical doctor. We talk about weirdness.

'EA likes cause areas that are neglected,' I say. 'But isn't there a trade-off there? Most of these causes are neglected because they're weird. In one of Singer's books he argues that if most people in the developed world donated to effective charities the problem of global poverty would be solved, and the amount of money needed from each person would be trivial. So he obviously wants EA to be a mainstream movement. But if the movement is increasingly about weird new cause areas, surely fewer people will join and that will undermine the non-weird causes like poverty?'

'Here's how some effective altruists think about weirdness,' one of the programmers replies. 'Imagine the organisation was around back in the mid nineteenth century, feeding the poor or doing whatever seemed impactful to them. Then people from the abolitionist movement or the early feminist movement come along and say "We think slavery is wrong" or "We think women should be able to vote". Well, those started off as weird, radical ideas. Should EA be an organisation that would have said "We're not going to support those things because they're weird"? Or should they have thought about them, applied the principles of the movement, and said, "Yes, we agree that slavery is wrong. That's an important cause area. Let's find the most impactful way to solve it." So the question then becomes: do you want EA to be that organisation today? If you rule new ideas out because they sound weird, then you'll risk ruling out future movements that have the chance to drastically improve the world.'

'But other people worry about weirdness points,' another programmer counter-explains. 'The theory is, each activist group has a set number of weirdness points they can spend before society discounts them. And most groups invest their points in a specific cause and try and shift it from weird to not weird. Gay rights activists didn't say, "We want gay marriage, but we also think everyone should be vegan and colonise Mars to protect the species from x-risk." And they probably wouldn't have succeeded if they did. If you're being meta-weird—weird across multiple domains, like EA—it makes it easier for society to dismiss you.'

'Does it?' the first programmer asks. 'EA didn't exist ten years ago. Now it's a global movement with billions of dollars in its charity ecosystem. Maybe weirdness is less of a problem than people think.'

By the standards of the global movement, the people at the New Zealand EA retreat are very normal. They're worried about x-risk, global poverty, animal suffering, feeding the world after the apocalypse: pretty vanilla stuff. The 2017 world conference in San Francisco featured more exotic cause areas, with many of the attendees on the margins of a movement that cherishes 'meta-contrarianism'. The radical fringe of the radical fringe.

Some of these more radical EAs are interested in qualia research. They reason that if most of our problems are about suffering, which is merely a state of consciousness, then you don't need to mess around trying to fix poverty or factory farming or anything else, because you can solve literally any problem by 'hacking consciousness directly'. Once you understand what consciousness is and how to recalibrate and reprogramme it, you (allegedly, according to the conference website's section about 'Qualia Computing') open up

> a full-fledged qualia economy: when people have spare resources and are interested in new states of consciousness, anyone good at mining the state-space for precious gems will have an economic advantage. In principle the whole economy may eventually be entirely based on exploring the state-space of consciousness and trading information about the most valuable contents discovered doing so.

Other effective altruists worry about 's-risk'. This is far more terrible than x-risk. If the human race or all sentient life were to be wiped out, that would be fairly bad. But what about a scenario in which some adverse outcome leads to suffering on a cosmic scale, vastly exceeding all suffering that has ever existed on Earth? What about that?

In 2010 the science fiction novelist Iain M. Banks published *Surface Detail*, describing a futuristic society that creates digital afterlives in which the mind-states of the state's political enemies are uploaded to virtual environments and tortured for all eternity. This is the kind of scenario s-risk activists worry about. What if an AGI alignment failure brought about such an outcome here on Earth? Or what if humans figure out how to create artificial sentient agents and do so in large numbers, and thoughtlessly inflict catastrophic suffering on them? Surely that would be worse than any of the suffering that exists in the world today. When you contemplate the sixty-four quadrillion future humans being tortured forever, the fates of the tiny handful of billions alive today looks rather trivial.

Although, maybe worrying about future s-risk is also trivial. Other effective altruists worry that the s-risk is already here, all around us: hard-coded into the universe itself. Where does suffering come from? Is it a by-product of consciousness, or is it a more fundamental property of existence? Can quarks and photons feel pain? Maybe the logical endpoint of effective altruism is to mitigate suffering by destroying the universe? The seminal article in this field, 'Is There Suffering in Fundamental Physics?' by Brian Tomasik, postulates:

> The main value (or disvalue) of intelligence would be to explore physics further and seek out tricks by which its long-term character could be transformed. For instance, if false-

vacuum decay did look beneficial with respect to reducing suffering in physics, civilization could wait until its lifetime was almost over anyway (letting those who want to create lots of happy and meaningful intelligent beings run their eudaimonic computations) and then try to ignite a false-vacuum decay for the benefit of the remainder of the universe (assuming this wouldn't impinge on distant aliens whose time wasn't yet up).

William MacAskill ended the 2017 conference by instructing the delegates to 'keep EA weird'.

*

The movement MacAskill co-founded has grown quickly. In 2009 he was one of a handful of Oxford students who agreed to live frugally and tithe to effective charities. By 2015 the global EA conference was being held at Google's Quad Campus in Mountain View, California. In 2017 Holden Karnofsky left GiveWell to become the executive director of the Open Philanthropy Project, an organisation founded to give away the bulk of the fortune belonging to Facebook co-founder Dustin Moskovitz and his wife Cari Tuna, currently valued at about US$11.3 billion. '"Open Philanthropy" is the most elite organisation in EA,' Catherine tells me. 'Research positions there are insanely competitive. Every effective altruist in the world wants to give away that money.'

The New Zealand chapter of EA also started in 2017, forming around the universities, a couple of Facebook groups, and delegations to Australian EA conferences. Catherine and the other organisers set up a charitable trust, and in the three years since then, it's moved approximately $600,000 to global health and poverty charities.

There are many, many criticisms of effective altruism. Most EAs have heard them all, and an H.G. Wells quote sometimes surfaces on EA-affiliated blogs: 'New and stirring things are belittled because if they are not belittled the humiliating question arises, "Why then are you not taking part in them?"' Effective altruism is open to criticism, but most EAs are sceptical of all the scepticism. Singer points out that when utilitarian logic conflicts with common-sense morality, people feel the need to justify their intuitive responses. He calls this 'intuition-chasing', and reminds us that we can't rely on common-sense morality to tell us how to be moral anymore. The world in which those intuitions evolved no longer exists.

One of Singer's most controversial ideas is that of 'the expanding moral circle'. The circle is an imaginary boundary that we draw around the beings that we care about, and whose suffering we empathise with, and who we will voluntarily make sacrifices for. Singer believes that the moral circle widens with the advance of reason—that it is now beginning to encompass other cultures, other peoples, non-human animals—but that you only get the widening of the circle if you think rationally about morality and suffering.

The most sustained critique of EA comes from the intellectual left. Sure, EA helps the child drowning in the pond, this argument goes, but it does not ask *why* the child is drowning. If the movement is to be truly effective, it must realise that capitalism is the cause of poverty and address that, instead of merely ameliorating its symptoms. Critiquing MacAskill's book in the *London Review of Books*, the philosopher Amia Srinivasan wrote:

Effective altruism, so far at least, has been a conservative movement, calling us back to where we already are: the world as it is, our institutions as they are. MacAskill does not address the deep sources of global misery—international trade and finance, debt, nationalism, imperialism, racial and gender-based subordination, war, environmental degradation, corruption, exploitation of labour—or the forces that ensure its reproduction. Effective altruism doesn't try to understand how power works, except to better align itself with it. In this sense it leaves everything just as it is. This is no doubt comforting to those who enjoy the status quo—and may in part account for the movement's success.

The effective altruists I speak to bristle with irritation when I put this argument to them. They want to eradicate global poverty and destroy the factory farming industry! That's hardly a movement dedicated to the status quo. But there is a broader critique there, which Singer anticipated back in 2009.

In *The Life You Can Save*, he wrote that you can be an anti-capitalist effective altruist, if you like, and you can try to convince the rest of the movement that ending capitalism is an impactful, neglected and tractable problem, and if you are persuasive then others in the movement will agree with you. But, Singer adds, being an anti-capitalist is not a moral get-out-of-jail-free card. It does not absolve you of your responsibility today, as a wealthy and fortunate person living in a world of terrible poverty. And, halfway through her review of MacAskill's book, Srinivasan admits that it inspired her to set up a donation to GiveDirectly, an EA charity that grants unconditional cash transfers to families living in poverty in East Africa.

It is true that EA would like to remain apolitical. Or, at least, as apolitical as a cause that wants to transfer vast sums of wealth to the developing world can remain. The logic is that EA aspires to be a broad church, but electoral politics is extremely polarising, and if the movement endorses specific parties or takes divisive positions it will alienate many potential members who don't agree with that endorsement, and that would be suboptimal. But people inside and outside EA wonder about this. Given that almost every cause area has a political dimension, can the overall movement remain politically uncommitted to the issues Srinivasan raises?

*

I wake early the next morning. It's the last day of the retreat. Most of the EAs stayed up late last night doing a quiz in which the questions were all Fermi estimates like, 'Guess the number of neurons in a chicken's brain.' Catherine's team won, the supertaster tells me when we meet on the gravel driveway and trudge up to the hall together, 'because Catherine doesn't have to make estimates. She just knows everything.'

While I'm preparing my breakfast, I meet Kyle, a tall guy with a large head and a big, unshaven jaw, who explains that he's 'in that weird place where you've finished your PhD but haven't defended it yet'.

'What's it on?'

'Using biomolecules to solve computational problems at the nanoscale.'

I pour him out a coffee and we talk about his work. 'Is the computation digital?' I ask. 'What's the bit?'

'The bit is the presence or absence of a wave in the nanoparticle. But I am really interested in non-digital computation.'

This is, randomly, an obscure topic I'm familiar with. 'I wrote an article about fluidic logic last year,' I tell him. 'Computers that use water instead of electricity.' We talk about the MONIAC hydraulic computer in the Reserve Bank Museum and the fluidic logic computers that the US military built during the Cold War.

'Why'd they build them?'

I tell him, 'Because fluidic circuits are immune to the electro-magnetic blast of a nuclear bomb.' But mentioning the apocalypse summons a flock of EAs into the hall.

'Building robust fluidic logic computers in the event of a nuclear exchange or solar storms could be an important cause area,' one announces.

'There's already an EA project team working on it in Amsterdam,' another replies. 'I can put you in touch with them.'

'That would be great. There's a 1.17 per cent chance per year of a nuclear war, so over a century the probability of a nuclear exchange rises to a near certainty.'

'I'm more worried about CRISPR. The commercial availability of gene-editing technologies lowers the minimum IQ needed to destroy the world by one point every eighteen months.'

My tea is steeping. I look out the window. The sun is coming up, and the tree directly outside is filled with tūī singing to each other.

Leftovers for lunch. The campground is partly deserted. Many people have already left. I eat outside with Catherine and a small group who have late planes or bus rides. We sit at the same picnic tables we sat at on the first day and I explain my EA-is-a-post-religious-religion theory to Catherine and Sophia. They attempt to feign interest until I interrupt my own stream of thought and say, 'But you don't have any music. Every organised religion needs music.'

Catherine replies, 'I can think of three types of EA music.'

'Is one of them composed by an algorithm?'

'I can think of four types of EA music.' She ticks them off on her fingers. 'There are EA choral groups in places like London and Boston. There's the hip-hop group Good Bayesian who rap about probabilistic reasoning. And there are GiveDirectly bands. Some of the charity's transfer recipients buy instruments and then make a living playing music. Some of their songs are tributes to universal basic income. And obviously there are Narrow AI compositions.'

'I've heard the "EA is a religion" argument before,' an engineer at an adjacent table remarks. 'Just because I give money to a charity and listen to a bunch of podcasts, I'm supposed to be a member of a religion? I don't follow.'

'I mean . . .' I hesitate and wonder, briefly, what do I mean? 'I mean that EA is a community with a distinct moral and intellectual framework.'

'Isn't that a description of most charities? Or political parties? Don't they all have their own moral framework? How is that religious?'

'I'm not talking about religion in the spiritual sense—'

'The meaning of a word is its use in the language,' one of the philosophers interrupts. 'When people talk about religion, they mean a spiritual faith. To me, effective altruism is about uncertainty. It's about trying to do good but realising that what you're doing might be wrong. It's about considering the evidence and changing your mind. Isn't that the opposite of faith?' There is a general murmur of agreement, and I realise I don't quite know what I'm trying to say and stop talking.

But here is what I would have said if I had been as quick-witted as the people I was trying to debate. Political parties do present themselves as moral and intellectual communities, but they're also coalitions of factions and vested interests and vehicles for personal ambition, and these tend to overwhelm everything else. A lot of people who get involved in politics are looking for a sense of purpose, a community, a coherent moral framework. Things that used to be adjacent to religion. We sense their absence in our lives. But if you're looking for meaning or a sense of purpose, you're probably not going to find it in political action. It asks very little of us: we vote for a party, maybe deliver their leaflets or share their content online, we despise their adversaries and blame them for ruining the world.

But EA, with its dietary taboos, tithing, apocalyptic obsessions, moral codes, complex texts and endless parable-like thought experiments, feels religious, as if the organisation is slowly but deliberately sketching out what an organised faith in a scientific culture looks like. It demands more of you. It pokes you in the chest and reminds you that, in global terms, you are a member of the 1 per cent. You, personally, have enormous wealth and privilege and you have the agency to make the world a better place. Singer has stopped telling people to give everything they can to charity, because most people respond to the drowning child scenario with cognitive dissonance and give nothing. In his most recent book, Singer suggests that we should be 'scalar utilitarians', who simply try to give more than the people around us. But he also reminds us there are still 700 million people living in absolute poverty. Many of them are children: about six million die every year. The child is still drowning.

*

Reasons and Persons opens with a famous quote by Nietzsche:

> Indeed, at hearing the news that 'the old god is dead', we philosophers and 'free spirits' feel illuminated by a new dawn;

our heart overflows with gratitude, amazement, forebodings, expectation—finally the horizon seems clear again, even if not bright; finally our ships may set out again, set out to face any danger; every daring of the lover of knowledge is allowed again; the sea, our sea, lies open again; maybe there has never been such an 'open sea'.

Nietzsche believed that most philosophers wasted the last two thousand years puzzling over religious moral systems—the noble lies based on gods and afterlives—and this means we've only just begun to solve the problem of what non-religious morality looks like. Parfit never found his flawless rational value system, but he thought that a partial solution lay in realising that our selves do not exist in any meaningful sense; that if we stop thinking about our future self as someone whose interests we need to protect above all else then we solve the coordination problem, because everyone always cooperates, so outcomes are rationally optimal. He admitted this was a difficult idea to accept, and that he himself struggled with it. But he was cheered by the notion that the Scottish enlightenment philosopher David Hume reached similar conclusions, as did the Buddha. One of the appendices in *Reasons and Persons* cites a Buddhist proverb:

The mental and the material are really here,
But here there is no human being to be found.
For it is void and merely fashioned like a doll.
Just suffering piled up like grass and sticks.

Parfit found this compatibility encouraging. His goal was to find an objective morality: one that spanned all cultures and all peoples. If the non-existence of the self had occurred to someone as separate in space and time from him as the Buddha, then that hinted at a possible universality. This was vital to Parfit, who believed that if morality was just an evolutionary strategy or a cultural preference—if there were no rational reason to save a child from drowning—then nothing would matter, and we would have no reason to try to decide how to live.

Some people relish the belief that we're heading towards the end of times, that humanity will be destroyed for our sins. There's always an apocalypse on the horizon. Parfit admits that an apocalypse is possible, but prefers to think of us as occupying the very beginning of history, only just starting to consider the problem of how to live together and live well. When we look back at previous generations and their values, we are often shocked by customs like slavery and torture and public executions, but Parfit was confident that subsequent generations will feel the same way about members of wealthy societies today, with our capacity to convince ourselves we are harmless torturers, and our failures to help the poorest people in the world. At the end of his second book, *On What Matters*, published six years before he died, he wrote:

> Life can be wonderful as well as terrible, and we shall increasingly have the power to make life good. Since human history may be only just beginning, we can expect that future humans, or supra-humans, may achieve some great goods that we cannot now even imagine. In Nietzsche's words, there has never been such a new dawn and clear horizon, and such an open sea.

*

It's time to clean the camp buildings. K and I are assigned to one of the dorms. It takes a long time, and K's optimal sweeping and mopping algorithm is too complicated for me to grasp. 'This is a disappointing way for your essay to end,' he observes. 'So boring. You should ask us to do something weird so you can finish on a climax.'

'You guys could sacrifice someone to your utility god. On a bonfire. That would be pretty climactic.'

He stops mopping the linoleum in order to consider this. 'We could. But how many readers would your essay have? How much pleasure would such an ending give them? It would have to be considerable to justify the pain of burning someone alive in order to maximise utility. What are your probabilistic priors?'

'I don't know how many people will read the essay,' I admit. 'Or how much pleasure they'd get from a first-hand account of a human sacrifice conducted by a group of philosopher nerds.'

K considers this. 'I don't think you've thought this through,' he says, and goes back to mopping the floor.

The Hunger and the Rain

I have to change buses at the mall. The next bus—the bus to the monastery—doesn't leave for another thirty minutes and although it's a sunny day it's windy and cold at the bus stop, so I wait inside the Westfield Queensgate shopping centre. Which is fine. I actually like malls. It's fashionable to hate them, and denounce them as symbols of civilisational decline, so I defend them on contrarian grounds. But I also just like them simply and unironically. I like the steady, unnatural light, the seasonless warmth. I find it relaxing to walk between the shops and happy shoppers, drifting about while waves of white noise from the chatter and air conditioning and background music wash over me. The escalators crowded with young families remind me of Larkin's vision of modernity as an uncomplicated utopia, with 'Everyone young going down the long slide / To happiness, endlessly'.

But today I am tired. I haven't been sleeping well: it's been a busy and stressful few months. The interior of the mall is bright, the music is too loud. The crowds of happy shoppers manifest as dark and ominous shapes, spectral, shimmering like migraine auras.

I need to eat, so I go to the food court on the mezzanine and order a Happy Meal, but while I'm waiting for it I lean on the balcony and sink into a fantasy about the mall of the post-apocalyptic future. The ground floor below me is flooded. The skylights in the roof have caved in. The heat is unbearable, and the air is thick with poisonous insects. The escalator has collapsed. It lies on its side, half submerged, covered in vines. The water is discoloured with algal blooms and coated with a shimmering chemical film. The shops are inhabited by monstrous crocodiles: they slumber in the drowned aisles of the supermarket and breed in the warm darkness of the derelict lingerie store.

I feel better once I've eaten, better still when I'm out of the mall and back on the bus, and I'm almost cheerful by the time I arrive at the monastery. Bodhinyanarama ('The Garden of Enlightened Knowing') is situated on the edge of Stokes Valley, a low-to-middle income commuter suburb in the Hutt Valley. It's only a minute's walk from the bus stop, but once you pass through the gate it feels very remote.

I walk up the driveway to the main building. This is a modern, two-storey, steel, concrete, wood and glass structure. I knock on the door, which is open, and offer a few 'Hello?'s into the silence, incrementally increasing my volume until I'm as loud as I think I can get, but there's no one around. Eventually I notice a card with my name on it lying on the kitchen counter. It welcomes me to Bodhinyanarama and reads, 'Turn this card around for a map of the monastery. Turn your attention around to discover your mind.'

I turn the card. The map shows me the way to my kuti, a Thai word meaning meditation hut. It leads me through the courtyard, past the cloister and meditation hall, then along a narrow trail through the bush, which zigzags up the slopes of a large hill. It takes about ten minutes to reach my hut, which is tiny: wood walls, glass and aluminium ranch sliding door, a corrugated iron roof. The interior has white plaster walls, a blue rug, a small bookshelf filled with Buddhist literature. The furniture consists of a single bed and a wooden chair. On a shelf sit a variety of Buddha statues in the South East Asian tradition: Buddhas who are young, slender, rather androgynous. Amidst them sits a framed black-and-white photograph of Ajahn Chah, the Thai monk who established the modern Thai Forest Tradition monastic movement.

The ranchslider leads out onto a wooden deck, and this looks back down the valley I've just walked up. The ridgelines of the lower hills overlap each other in a series of intersecting V-shapes, recursing away into the afternoon haze. The roofs of some of the other huts are visible just above the treeline further down the valley. The birdsong is very loud but if I concentrate I can still hear the faint sound of traffic.

I've stayed here before, about six months ago. I stayed in this same hut. But when I told a friend I was coming back here she made fun of me. 'Why do you keep annoying the Buddhists? Why don't you go have your midlife crisis in a Catholic Monastery?'

'Because I'm not a Catholic.'

'You're not a Buddhist either, Danyl. You've just read a few books about it.'

I thought about taking her advice. I even looked at a few websites of Catholic monasteries, and they looked nice enough. But nothing ever came of it, and as I move the chair out onto the deck and sit down on it to meditate I'm glad I ignored my friend, because this place is just what I need.

I meditate for most of the afternoon. But I get cold and a

little lonely at about 5pm, so I walk back down the hill to the kitchen. There's a woman there. She's small, extremely thin, in late middle-age with short, dark hair. I will call her S. She's one of the lay residents: a small group of people who live at the monastery and help run it, but who haven't been ordained as monks or nuns. She sits me down in the glass-fronted hall running along the side of the main building and asks me if I've stayed here before.

'Yes,' I reply. 'Earlier this year. I think you were away travelling.'

'So you know the rules of the monastery?'

'Yes.'

'The precepts.'

'Yes.'

'And the schedule?'

'Yes, yes.'

'And you know about the festival on Sunday? Kathina?'

'The what?'

There are five ordained monks living at Bodhinyanarama at the time of my visit, and no nuns. The monks live in huts on the opposite side of the valley from mine. They spend most of their days meditating and studying. They're bound by a code of discipline which regulates almost every aspect of their lives, and includes not handling money, not driving, not preparing meals, and only eating food that has been offered to them. There are 227 rules for monks—but 311 for nuns, many of them forbidding the nuns from being depraved, consorting with lusting men, sympathising with women thieves, or walking through long grass while not wearing any underwear. The lay residents perform much of the day-to-day running of the place, the tasks the monks are forbidden to do.

For the last three lunar months, S explains, the monastery

has observed Vassa, a state of retreat corresponding to the rainy season in South and South East Asia. This year it's run from June to October, and the residents of the monastery have spent that time fasting and meditating. Now Vassa is over and they mark this in four days' time with Kathina, a celebration with ceremonies and a large feast.

'Have you come to Bodhinyanarama for solitude and meditation?'

'That was my plan.'

She nods. 'There will be hundreds of people here for Kathina,' she explains. 'People from Thailand. Sri Lanka. Cambodia. Laos. Vietnam. It will still be somewhat quiet in your kuti,' she concedes, before adding, 'but there is a huge amount of work to do to prepare for the festival. And you will have to help.'

'I'd also hoped to speak to the Abbot, Ajahn Kusalo.'

'Ajahn is very busy.' (Ajahn is an honorific, a little like calling someone 'sensei'; it denotes monks who have passed at least ten Vassa in a monk's robes.) 'He is arranging the festival. Ceremonies at other temples. Meeting with ambassadors. The best time to speak to Ajahn is . . .' She pauses to think about this for a moment then concludes, 'The best time to speak to Ajahn is April.'

'April? As in . . . the month of April? Six months from now?'

'Other times he is on self-retreat. Or travelling. April is best.'

Bodhinyanarama was founded in 1985, but if you stand in the central courtyard in just the right spot you can enjoy the illusion that it's been there for a thousand years. The courtyard is gravel and stone. Near the centre, mounted on a plinth, is an engraved brass bell which is rung to signal meal times and other gatherings. At the far end stands a tall brass statue of the Buddha depicted in the Thai tradition: slender, young, draped in a robe, standing atop a lotus flower. A wall of trees runs opposite the main building. Some of them are kōwhai, and they're in bloom, and the yellow blossoms lie scattered around the bases of the statue and the bell, unnaturally bright against all the grey stone.

Behind the statue is the cloister. This is a wooden square designed for walking meditation. Circular pillars hold up a wooden roof which runs around the sides. The large square space in the centre is normally open to the sky. Today it's covered by a large canvas tent: one of the preparations for the festival. Beyond the cloister lies the meditation hall: a temple with wood-panelled walls and a high white portico with a stylised wheel in the centre.

S returns to her hut, and there's no one else around, so I spend the late afternoon in the library. This is a separate, modestly sized building not far from the courtyard. Most of the books are, unsurprisingly, about Buddhism, although there's a handful of works on literature, philosophy, new age mysticism: Martin Heidegger's *Introduction to Metaphysics* is here, along with books by people like Krishnamurti and Eckhart Tolle. Roughly half of the books are in English; the rest are in Thai, Sinhalese, Pali. There's an old-fashioned card catalogue. Peacock statuettes on the desk, a reclining Buddha on one shelf. The main window looks out onto a sheer wall of native bush. There's a photo of the Dalai Lama on the back of the door.

There's no one here, which surprises me. The library is the only place in the monastery that is heated—they keep it warm to prevent the books from getting damp—and the first time I stayed here many of the other guests naturally gravitated here in the early evenings. This became a rather lively social event, until the Abbot found out about it and called us all before him. By staying in his monastery, he reminded us, we'd agreed to abide by the eight precepts, the fourth of which was to refrain from incorrect speech, and this included gossip and idle chatter, which was what most of those conversations in the library consisted of. After that we still went back there in the evenings because we were cold, but we read in companionable silence.

Tonight I have the library to myself. But I miss the gossip and companionable silence so I return to my kuti. It's about five thirty. The sun won't set for hours, but in the bush it's already gloomy, twilit. The trail is narrow, running between dead ferns, rotting ponga trunks, vines twisting to waist height. A stream runs down the valley, fed by innumerable tributaries. The monks use the sound of the water as a meditation object.

Here are the precepts you agree to live by when you stay at the monastery:

1. To refrain from destroying living creatures (harmlessness: not intentionally taking the life of any living creature).
2. To refrain from taking that which is not given (trustworthiness).
3. To refrain from any kind of intentional sexual behaviour (celibacy).
4. To refrain from incorrect speech (avoiding false, abusive or malicious speech and idle chatter).
5. To refrain from intoxicating drink and drugs, which lead to carelessness (sobriety).
6. To refrain from eating at wrong times (restraint: not eating after midday).

7. To refrain from beautification, entertainment, and adornment (restraint: not seeking distraction, not playing radios and music, and dressing modestly).
8. To refrain from lying on a high or luxurious sleeping place (alertness: refraining from overindulgence in sleep).

The first five of these are the day-to-day values you're supposed to observe if you're a lay Buddhist, i.e. you follow the dharma but you are not a monk, with the proviso that lay Buddhists don't have to be celibate; they're just supposed to avoid sexual misconduct. But actual celibacy, along with precepts six to eight, are the rules at a monastery. So gossiping with the other guests put me in breach of precept four. Killing a mosquito that bit me when I was meditating might have put me in breach of precept one, although the question of whether killing mosquitos is bad karma is a subject of endless debate among philosophically inclined Buddhists.

But the precept I worried about before my first visit was number six: eating at the wrong times. Because at Bodhinyanarama the wrong time is almost all the time. You're allowed a light breakfast at 6:30am and a main meal at 10:30am, and nothing after that until breakfast the next day. This is very different from my diet at home, which involves breakfast, a midmorning snack, and then lunch followed by a series of rolling snacks during the mid and late afternoon, culminating in a large dinner supplemented by some post-dinner snacks or dessert.

This is a terrible diet and I'm very overweight, and I've spent years attempting to change what I eat and when I eat it, and all of those attempts have failed. So staying at a place where I would eat only one proper meal was, I worried, doomed to be a miserable ordeal in which I constantly felt hungry and thought about nothing but food. But what I found during my first visit was that I was never really hungry here at all.

Sometimes, when I'm upset about my weight—which is most of the time—I print out papers on the psychology and biochemistry of diet and compulsive eating. I read them over lunch and the science is fairly bleak. Being a person prone to obesity is about 70 per cent genetic. There's no single gene responsible: about 150 genes, transcription factors and other gene products regulate appetite, weight and body shape, controlling everything from hunger to digestion to stomach receptors to regulation and activation of the hedonic pathways in the brain—the neural circuits that reward us with feelings of pleasure whenever we do anything pleasurable.

There's a classic study in the obesity and food addiction literature. You take a selection of obese and non-obese people, show them pictures of chocolate milkshakes to activate their anticipation, then stick their heads in an MRI scanner, then give them the milkshake. The obese participants showed greater activation of the reward circuitry prior to drinking the milkshake, when they were looking forward to it, and much lower activation when they actually drank it. Obese people tend to anticipate and crave food more but enjoy it less. And that incentivises us to eat larger quantities of food, ideally food packed with sugar, fat and salt, because that's what gets us closest to the feelings of pleasure that non-obese people get from eating normally.

Humans aren't supposed to be overweight. We evolved to be hunter-gatherers in the midpoint of the food chain. So our bodies have multiple oversight and feedback systems designed to keep us at healthy weights. Even if you're genetically inclined to crave food more, we still have biochemical and neurological regulators upstream from those cravings, signalling for us to exercise more or eat less if our body fat goes above a certain window. But modern food products—milkshakes, Happy Meals—have been brilliantly designed to circumvent those controls so that our jaws don't need to do much work. The act of chewing sends the brain signals of satiety. If we've chewed and salivated a lot then the brain assumes we've had enough to eat, and it tells us to stop eating. Most of the junk food I consume is 'prechewed and pre-salivated', to use the wonderfully disgusting terminology of the nutritional literature, by which they mean it's been processed and has a high water content, designed to be tasted and swallowed without chewing, so I can just go on eating more and more of it.

Why don't I get hungry at the monastery? I'm still not sure, but I know the answer isn't willpower. Willpower is a controversial subject, but many neuroscientists are beginning to suspect it doesn't exist, The reward pathways in our brain tell us what to do because it feels pleasurable and we do it, or it doesn't so we don't. I don't like drinking alcohol, while some people can't stop drinking it, and this has nothing to do with willpower or choice and everything to do with neurochemistry: different receptors in our brains responding to different stimuli and rewards. Something about life at the monastery changes the incentive structure of my reward system.

The air in the meditation hall is scented and cool. The light is dim. The floor is highly polished wood. At the back of the room is the shrine: a large statue of a meditating Buddha surrounded by fresh flowers, candles, incense. The resident monks sit on a raised platform directly in front of the shrine. Five of them wear dark brown robes; two of them wear white. The monks in white are much younger than the others. Facing the monks and the statue, sitting cross-legged on meditation cushions, are the two lay residents, four resident guests and two casual visitors who've come for the evening puja—the chanting and meditation ceremony. Puja is a very old Hindu word meaning an act of worship. At the monastery this involves two hours of chanting and meditation every night, beginning at 7pm, and another hour and a half every morning at 5:15am. Attendance at both is mandatory.

It's very, very quiet in here. You can hear the birds and the stream, and you can hear my footsteps as I hurry in, a little late because I've walked down the trail by torchlight and it took me longer than I expected. I take a seat on the floor and pick up a book of chants, and remember that the Abbot hates lateness, instructing his guests, 'In my monastery five minutes early is right on time.'

The Abbot, Ajahn Kusalo, sits in the middle of the monks, directly beneath the Buddha statue. He's in his late sixties but looks about ten years younger. He is bald and clean-shaven. He has a manner of quick, amused intelligence and self-confidence but also a faint air of menace. If you bumped into him in a bar you'd apologise very quickly.

He announces the chants and suttas we'll sing tonight and then we begin. We chant in Pali, the sacred and liturgical language of Theravada Buddhism, widely spoken in the Indian subcontinent from the fifth to the first century BCE. It's probably close to the language the actual Buddha spoke, and it's what the first Buddhist scriptures were written in, and I find it very hard to read aloud and sing along to. It has long compound words and non-European inflections on almost every syllable. Here is the opening of the *Dhammapada*, the best-known Buddhist scripture:

Manopubbaṅgamā dhammā, manoseṭṭhā manomayā;
Manasā ce paduṭṭhena, bhāsati vā karoti vā,
Tato naṁ dukkhaṁ anveti, cakkaṁ'va vahato padaṁ

The monks sing loudly, the lay residents less loudly, the other guests are quieter and less confident, the visitors mumble along, and I keep mispronouncing things and losing my place and produce almost no sound at all. At the end of each chant we bow towards the shrine, and at the end of it all we bow towards the monks while the monks bow towards the Abbot.

The first time I stayed here, I had a problem with all this chanting and bowing. I'd made peace with the idea of Buddhism as a philosophical tradition, an empirical study of psychology and meditation, but when you're singing in a dead language and bowing to a shrine, you're no longer in philosophical territory. You're obviously worshipping. When Maggie picked me up at the end of my first stay and asked me how it was, I replied, 'It was interesting,' and added in a disapproving tone, 'but a lot of it was religious.' And she replied, in a slightly pained voice, 'It's a monastery.'

After the chanting we meditate for an hour and a half, then a bell rings and the ceremony ends. You're supposed to maintain Noble Silence between the evening and morning puja, which means that I'm not supposed to talk to anyone until 6:30am tomorrow. But the Abbot speaks to us for a few minutes after the session, and when he's finished the other monks whisper to each other, so I feel like I have a brief window to speak with the Abbot.

I try to stand and find that my feet have lost all sensation. I've been sitting on them for almost two hours. I have no muscle control below my knees. I wobble across the room, throwing my arms out for balance, attempting to intercept the Abbot as he heads towards the monk's exit at the back of the hall but veering off into unplanned trajectories as my legs malfunction. He pauses to watch my progress, an expression of polite amusement on his face, until I stand before him.

'I don't know if you remember me?' I say. 'I stayed here about six months ago. We talked about meditation and mood disorders and monastic life?'

'Oh?'

'And I remember being very interested in your ideas, but I didn't note any of them down and I don't quite remember much of what you said.'

'Oh.'

'So I know this is a busy weekend and a bad time, but I'm here until Sunday, and if you could find just a few minutes to talk to me? And I'll take notes this time?'

I wait. The other monks have left the hall. The Abbot looks me up and down and says, 'Yeah, I remember you.'

I sleep badly. The bed in the kuti is hard (precept eight: 'refrain from lying on a high or luxurious sleeping place') and I've left the curtain over the ranchslider open because I have a romantic notion of being woken by the sunrise. But the streetlights from the suburb stain the low clouds a luminous chemical orange. The light keeps me awake, but I'm too tired to get up and close the curtain, and I finally fall asleep around midnight. At 2am the rain starts. It's very loud on the metal roof and maddeningly random and arrhythmic, as if it's deliberately beating out of time just to keep me awake. I read by torchlight until 5am then walk very carefully down the trail, which is already turning into a stream.

I like the morning puja. It's the same as the evening one, only with the sequence reversed: first meditation, then chanting.

But there's a sense of ritual and community I get from walking through the dawn to the candlelit hall, then sitting in silence and meditating for a great deal longer than I have the time or patience for in day-to-day life. I even sort of like the chanting.

After the puja we do chores. It's about twenty-two hours since my Happy Meal, and under ordinary circumstances I would now be hungry and angry. But I'm fine. S tells me to sweep the polished concrete floor of the glass-fronted hallway in the main building, and while I do this a group of monks sweep the courtyard. The sun is rising, lighting up the grey stones, and then the wind picks up and sends down a storm of kōwhai blossoms, spinning them around the monks in their brown and white robes, who stand inside the vortex of yellow petals, regarding them with bemused calm.

We eat a light breakfast—muesli—and while I'm washing the dishes I talk to B, one of the trainee monks. He's Australian, in his late twenties. Shaved head and clean-shaven. I wash and he dries, because the kitchen is large and I don't know where anything goes.

'So what's your official title here? Are you a novice? Can I call you that?'

'My official title is Anagārika. It means homeless meditator. That's my status for a year, and then they can ordain me as a monk.'

'What did you do before you came here?'

'I've mostly just lived in Buddhist monasteries,' he replies. 'But right before I came here I spent a month living on the street in Sydney. You know, living without possessions, and meditating. So I was literally a homeless meditator. I wanted to have that experience and bring it into my calling as a monk.'

This is less odd than it sounds. Buddhism has a long tradition of monks living as mendicants, or beggars. It's how the Buddha himself started out.

'The first monk I ever met was mendicant,' B explains. 'He was a lawyer and he renounced all his wealth and walked from Sydney to the northern tip of Queensland, begging and teaching the dharma.'

'Was it scary being homeless in Sydney?'

'Yeah. I mean, I was lucky, nothing bad happened. But it was scary. And very humbling. I got advice from another Buddhist I knew who was homeless and who meditated on the street. I was going to sleep in the park, because I thought I needed privacy to sleep. But he told me that the park was too dangerous, and that the safest place to sleep is the footpath of a busy street where there are lots of people around. And he showed me where I could get free showers, and a restaurant that fed the homeless. I ended up volunteering there.'

'Was it hard to sleep on the street like that?'

'It was. I'd meditated for years, and I thought that I'd triumphed over my pride and my sense of self and all that stuff. And sleeping on the street in front of people taught me that I still had so much pride in me.'

'Are there lots of people in Sydney who are homeless for spiritual reasons?'

'Not really. If you're homeless it's generally because you're crazy or you have drug and alcohol problems.' He smiled. 'There's no group of enlightened beings living on the streets. It's a romantic idea though.'

'Maybe there are,' I reply. 'Maybe they're the secret rulers of the world.'

B shakes his head. 'It's hard to meditate in the city,' he says. 'I tried, and I ended up walking around talking to myself, reciting poetry. The Buddha tells us that it's better to sleep in the forest than meditate in the city.'

*

The monastery is surrounded by a network of trails through the bush. Some of these lead to the kutis or the stupa. (A stupa is a burial mound, prominent in the Buddhist architectural tradition; at Bodhinyanarama it is large and white, sitting on the promontory of one of the hills.) But most of the trails are just walking trails, and they're used by people to jog along or walk their dogs.

The period between the end of breakfast and the main meal at 10:30am is the work period. On my previous visit I spent my first chore period doing trail duty. This was rather pleasant. You take some clippers and machetes and spades and head up into the bush, and you can pair up with someone and chat with them, or just take a section on your own and cut back branches and clear culverts of mud and leaves.

On the second morning of that visit, though, one of the lay residents stopped me before I reached the trail, telling me, 'You work with Ajahn Kusalo today.' I felt rather privileged to be singled out to spend the morning with the head of the monastery and I didn't register the expressions of sympathy on the faces of the other visitors, who had all been there much longer than I had, and who hurried on up the path away from me.

The lay resident led me to a collection of kutis near the main courtyard. These were two-storey buildings, one separate room atop another. Ajahn Kusalo waited for me in the gutted bottom level of one of them, dressed in his brown robe and a pair of black gumboots, holding a large shovel. He stood between a large steel wheelbarrow and a huge mound of fresh earth.

'I've stripped out these walls,' he explained, 'because the building is damp and it needs to be properly insulated, ventilated and clad. Do you know how to do any of that?'

'Not remotely.'

'What are you like at mixing concrete?'

'I've never done it before. Maybe I'm really good at it.'

'Right.' He handed me the shovel. 'We've had a bit of subsidence overnight.' He pointed at the waist-high mound of sodden clay, which had slipped down from the bank behind the kuti. 'This all needs to be shovelled into the barrow and hauled away. And while we work we can talk.'

To my eyes, shifting the clay looked like a good day's effort, maybe two, and I took the shovel and set to work, slowly but steadily. To the Abbot, however, shifting the clay was merely one of many tasks to be completed that morning and it had to be done as soon as possible so that we could move on to the other tasks, which were even more difficult.

So we shovelled clay, and talked, and then we mixed concrete, and after that we chipped wooden tiles off a concrete base and talked. Because I am a fat, unfit, unskilled man and I found the work so exhausting, I remember little of what was said. We talked about meditation, of course, and Buddhism, and the nature of reality and the nature of mind. And at first I thought it was charming to discuss philosophy with a real monk while shovelling mounds of dirt. But then I formed blisters on my hands, and by the time they popped and started bleeding we were only about ninety minutes into the two-and-a-half hour chore period, and I wasn't sure I could go on.

I showed my lacerated hands to the Abbot. Compassion is a core tenet of Buddhism and he'd vowed to follow a strict code of monastic discipline, so I figured he was obligated to let me off work for the rest of the morning. But he barely glanced at my wounds. Instead he said, 'Just wipe the blood on the grass. Your hands'll scab up pretty fast.'

But one moment from that conversation stuck in my mind. I made a sharp comment about the chanting during the puja and the merits of atheism and reason versus superstition, and the Abbot, damping down a dirt floor where he intended to pour down concrete, replied, 'Singing brings people together. That's not the only reason we do it but it's one of them. You can tell yourself that it's irrational while you're living your life in a rational and scientific way'—he fluttered his hand dismissively—'if you like. And maybe you are and maybe you aren't. But if you want to build a community, then the values and practices of that community have to be meaningful to a broader group of people than just sceptical intellectuals.'

It's a comment that came back to me a few months later. I was at work going through my emails and one of my Google alerts for neuroscience and depression served me up a paper on the mental health effects of group singing. The study showed that singing along with a large group of people releases endorphins and oxytocin: neurotransmitters which make you more relaxed and less stressed and boost feelings of social inclusion and cohesion. The timing of the music literally synchronises the heartbeats of the singers.

*

I was once an ardent and evangelical atheist. Back in my twenties I was very influenced by the New Atheist movement, which rose to prominence in the early 2000s. This was a sort of all-star team of ultra-sceptical intellectuals—Richard Dawkins, Sam Harris, Christopher Hitchens—who regarded religion as the main problem with the world. Mystical beliefs and non-rational thinking were the reasons bad things happened. This was after September 11 and the US and UK-led invasion of Iraq, twin catastrophes that the New Atheists claimed were religiously motivated. At the same time there was this ferocious cultural debate about evolution. Should it be taught in schools? Should 'intelligent design' be taught alongside it? I was studying undergraduate biology when this great cultural war broke out, and I strongly identified with the biology-science-atheism-reason side of this conflict, so I read a lot of books by New Atheist authors and spent a lot of time arguing with fundamentalist Christians about evolutionary theory on the internet.

In retrospect most of this was a waste of time, but I learned a lot from Richard Dawkins' science writing, and the more I meditated the more I found myself thinking about Dawkins' first book, *The Selfish Gene*.

Dawkins was—and still is—the most evangelical of the New Atheists. He's a rather disreputable figure nowadays. This is mostly his own fault. He's intolerant, strident, given to conspiratorial twitter rants denouncing Muslims and feminists. Shortly after my first visit to the monastery I reread *The Selfish Gene*, and a few people who saw me reading it on campus asked—with some distaste—why I was reading Dawkins. Isn't he problematic? Hasn't he been cancelled?

Which is a shame, because *The Selfish Gene* is one of the great popular science books. Going back to it nearly twenty years later I was surprised by how well it holds together. It's a book about genetics published in 1976, long before the human genome was sequenced, and it's outdated in parts, of course, but most of it stands up. And it's more than a science book. It's a philosophical book, a book about the problem of evil, the problem that Dawkins now believes is caused by religious belief, but which his own book suggests has little or nothing to do with this at all. It's a book that tells us more about life and rationality than the author thinks it does.

This shouldn't surprise us. Dawkins was a young zoology lecturer when he wrote *The Selfish Gene*. It was his first book and it's a masterpiece of the genre it helped invent: the science bestseller that unites a range of discoveries and ideas and packages them all into a coherent narrative. The gene-centric view of evolution is now inseparable from Dawkins, but the book is a synthesis of ideas from other mid-twentieth-century biologists: George Williams, Bill Hamilton, John Maynard Smith, Robert Trivers, George Price. Dawkins brings them all together, along with findings from hundreds of papers and studies. The result is a synthesis now known as 'selfish gene theory'.

The title was a mistake. Even Dawkins admits this now. His publisher preferred 'The Immortal Gene', because genes aren't selfish in the sense that humans or other animals can be selfish. They have no desires; they're just sequences of chemical information. More importantly—and this is one of the major themes of Dawkins' book—genes cooperate, because cooperation is rational. They'll behave altruistically if it is in their interest to do so, which it often is.

But they are immortal, and that points towards one of the most challenging ideas in the book. Some critics thought that by talking about 'selfish genes' Dawkins was making assertions about human nature, that he'd claimed humans are innately selfish and individualistic. And of course that isn't true. We see evidence of altruism and cooperation everywhere in human life. What the book is *actually* saying is far more disturbing. Instead of speaking to human nature, *The Selfish Gene* argues that humans are peripheral and unimportant. We are fleeting. The primary actors on Earth are the genes that build us. We are their temporary hosts. They use us to replicate themselves across space and transport themselves through time. 'We are survival machines,' Dawkins wrote, 'robot vehicles blindly programmed to preserve the selfish molecules known as genes.'

Prior to Dawkins, most biologists thought of DNA as a tool that humans and other organisms use to propagate our species. They're a means to an end, like our eyes or our lungs. Our eyes see, our lungs breathe, our DNA functions as a code repository and instruction kit to build the proteins that do all of this. But we don't use the genes, Dawkins argues: they use us. They build us, then use our bodies to accumulate energy and resources in order to make new copies of themselves. Eventually we die and they survive.

This explains an awful lot about the natural world. Why are some organisms multicellular? Why are some insects social? Why do parents care for their children? Why do members of flocks and herds and hives and societies help one another? Why do we suffer? Because the genes are not individualistic. They exist in multiple copies across multiple organisms, and they maximise their overall replication, not the happiness or the survival of the organisms they happen to inhabit. We're designed and built by processes that are indifferent to our suffering and that consider us disposable.

The genes began as replicators: simple chemical arrangements that could make copies of themselves. They came into existence about four billion years ago. No one knows how they first self-assembled, or where (mineral-rich volcanic vents on the ocean bed are strong contenders). The replicators don't *want* to copy themselves and they're not selfish, or unselfish, or sentient in any conceivable way. It just works out that the laws of chemistry allow for certain sequences of atoms—mostly carbon, hydrogen and nitrogen—to arrange themselves in certain configurations, which copy themselves if they have access to energy and raw materials, both of which were abundant in the warm, chemical-rich environment of the oceans of the early Earth.

And everything flows from that. Over time the replicators form different arrangements, not intentionally, just randomly, and eventually one of them assembles into a pattern that also allows it to build additional structures that help it obtain more resources, or protect itself, which allows it to build yet more copies. And over time the copies build cell walls, flagella to move around, enzymes to make the copying process more efficient. And, again, none of this is intentional. Everything is an accident. Random configurations of atoms come together. Most of them do nothing, drift apart, but when you're dealing with planet-sized oceans and geological timescales, highly unlikely accidents happen relatively frequently. The complexity of the replicators aggregates. They band together. Form colonies. Specialise. At some point we can talk about organisms. Bacteria. Plants. Animals. All of these are molecular robots built by the replicators to facilitate the self-copying process. Some of them assemble in ways that allow them to capture energy from sunlight, and they use that energy to copy themselves, and others consume those organisms, and some of them consume the consumers.

The copying process always generates errors in the chemical sequences, and this is how evolution happens. Most of the errors mean that the organism—the host, the robot—fails to survive, but this is of total indifference to the genes. Every now and then a copying error leads to an improvement. This is also a matter of indifference, everything is, but the improvements proliferate, outcompeting inferior configurations.

In one of his later books, Dawkins shows how the evolutionary process explores genetic space. This is a hypothetical universe—what mathematicians call a 'vector space'—in which the errors in the copying allow the replicators to randomly iterate through different sequences of information. These strands of chemical codes create structures in the actual universe; that is, they create organisms in which the replicators can live and compete with each other. Genetic space is like Borges' Infinite Library. Most sequences and gene combinations are meaningless; most of the paths they explore lead nowhere—death for the organism, maybe extinction for the species. But a few lead to clearings that open out into vast new spaces of life. Internal complexity. Multicellularity. Sensory systems that can detect the environment. Nervous systems that can predict the internal and external states of the organism, i.e. brains.

Brains endow the survival vehicles with a certain degree of autonomy. They can make choices, and this opens up the possibility of hosts doing things the replicators don't want them to. An incentive alignment problem. So the replicators find a new pathway in genetic space and they invent pleasure and pain. This allows them to programme their vehicles effectively, ensuring that we're always maximising their utility, not ours. As hosts, we work hard to keep the interior of our cells early-Earth-like: aqueous, warm, salty, anaerobic. The conditions in which the replicators evolved.

Every organism on the planet is a survival mechanism for the replicators. We're tools for capturing energy and resources and replicating the chemical sequences encoded in our DNA, passing them on into the future. We're a gene's way to make copies of itself, so that those copies can make more copies, and those copies can make more copies. Forever.

*

The chore period begins at 8am. We aren't on trail duty today. Nor are we mixing concrete or shovelling clay. Today is Friday and the Kathina Festival is Sunday, and there is a lot of work to be done between then and now.

The first job is to put down carpets in the concrete space in the centre of the cloister, because that's where most of the visitors will sit. There are large canvas bags containing rugs and felt underlays stored away in the attic above the meditation hall. This is accessed via a narrow set of stairs leading to a narrow step-ladder. We form a human chain, guests and monks and homeless meditators, all ferrying dozens of heavy rolled-up rugs down to the ground floor and around the sides of the hall. The underlay and carpets are all different shapes and sizes, and they all fit into the space if you arrange them in a very precise geometric pattern, which Ajahn Kusalo knows to the exact millimetre.

As soon as we've finished arranging the carpets, the rain intensifies. There are leaks in the tent over the cloister. We've put down buckets to catch the drips but this new deluge sends a cascade of water spilling down around the central tent pole. There are lights mounted on the pole, about five metres up, and the streams of water pouring over them glitter in the radiance. One of the monks says, 'It looks like it's raining light.'

'Those are just low-voltage LED bulbs,' the Abbot growls. 'But they're still connected to mains power and I want to electrocute as few guests as possible this year.' He thinks for a moment. 'We'll set up a tarp,' he decides. 'Above the lights. We'll tension it to catch the leaks and funnel them, then suspend a bucket beneath it.' He starts pointing at guests and monks. 'Go get the large black tarpaulin from the attic. Someone else get the ladder. The rest of you go get the prayer flags and start hanging them up around the walls. Not you, Danyl. I want you to search the attic for a bag of garlands and hang them around the Buddha statues in the shape of a heart.' Everyone scrambles to obey, and the Abbot rubs his hands together, announcing happily, 'I'm just a frustrated holiday camp decorator at heart.'

The Abbot carries a saffron-coloured handbag around with him most of the time. It is filled with various tools and knives, and he also wears a tourist's fanny-pack around his waist containing even more knives, and smaller tools, and he produces and uses an assortment of these while he ties his rainproof tarp into position from atop a tall aluminium ladder. Down below, B and I keep the ladder steady.

While we wait I ask B, 'Did you try out any other religions before you committed to this one? Did you stay at, say, a Catholic monastery?'

'Not really. Maybe I should have. I visited a Greek Orthodox monastery once. The Theravada monastery I lived at in Sydney was in the middle of a national park, and there was this Greek Orthodox community about two hours' walk away. So I walked over there one day.'

'How'd it go?'

He makes a face. 'Some people say that the different faiths approach the truth from different directions. You know—we're all climbing the same mountain. So I tried to find common ground with the Orthodox monks. I said: "You guys like asceticism, we like asceticism. You've renounced the sensual world. We've renounced the sensual world." But they just kept bringing everything back to Jesus.'

'Do you worry about renouncing the sensual world?'

'I've spent a lot of time this year thinking about that. It's like: Buddhism is supposed to be the solution to suffering, but why reject the nice things in life? Why reject pleasure?'

'What've you come up with?'

He tips his head to one side. 'What do you think the answer is?'

'Doesn't the Buddha teach that the desire for pleasure leads to suffering? That sensual pleasure is like scratching an insect bite? It feels good in the short term but really just aggravates things?'

'That's pretty much it,' he replies. 'But the metaphor the Buddha uses in the suttas is more graphic. He compares sensual pleasure to a leper scratching at a sore.'

I nod. This makes sense. If I was the Buddha, trying to convince people to take an oath of celibacy, I'd go with the stronger image.

*

In 1975, one year before *The Selfish Gene* was published, the evolutionary biologist George Price committed suicide. Price's collaborative work with the geneticist John Maynard Smith was at the heart of Dawkins' book. He derived the Price equation: the mathematical description of how a trait that increases fitness will spread through any reproducing population. It's one of the central formulae in modern evolutionary theory.

Price also pioneered the application of game theory to evolutionary biology. He was interested in altruism. Why did some organisms help each other while others did not? He used his formula and its derivations to show that most of our behaviour, for good or evil—and the behaviour of plants, fish, insects, bacteria, basically every living thing—is driven by the calculations of the replicators as competing players in strategic games. Genes, cells, animals: the more genetically similar they are, the more likely they are to cooperate. So it's rational for a gene to sacrifice an individual organism to protect further copies of itself. But genes will also defect from positive-sum coalitions if there's an advantage to an individual gene. And this is where things get bleak.

Dawkins asks us to imagine a hypothetical nest filled with baby birds. The mother bird has a worm, and she's trying to figure out which baby to feed. The babies signal their hunger by chirping at their mother. In an ideal world, the noise of the chirping will signal each baby's real level of hunger, so that the mother can simply give the worm to the baby that needs it most.

But resources are scarce. Sometimes there won't be enough food for every baby bird to survive. If one bird chirps loudly no matter how hungry it is, it will get more food and be more likely to live than its siblings; the mutation in a gene or combination of genes that causes the loud chirping is thus more likely to persist. And because of that, this gene will be more likely to spread throughout the species until all the baby birds in a nest chirp loudly no matter how hungry they are, with the rewards going to birds that chirp even more loudly, until they reach some maximal point. Maybe they get so loud they attract predators; maybe the energy consumed by chirping is greater than the energy that can be obtained by food. Now every baby bird is chirping loudly for no gain, because everyone else is doing it, and there's no way to dial it back. It's an outcome that's bad for the species and even worse for the individuals, but you get there anyway because the genes are blindly following the logic of the non-iterated prisoner's dilemma, defecting whenever there's short-term gain to be had.

Price and Maynard Smith refer to scenarios like the maximally chirping baby birds as an evolutionarily stable strategy, or ESS. It's another somewhat misleading name. An ESS isn't stable for the species or even, ultimately, for the gene; it's stable in the sense that it can't be invaded by an alternative strategy. If birds that chirp less than average evolve, they get no food and die, and the chirpless gene dies too. So it's possible for a species to arrive at an evolutionarily stable strategy that drives it to extinction, a process that's referred to variously as 'evolutionary suicide', 'Darwinian extinction', 'runaway selection to self-extinction', and 'evolutionary collapse'. We think of species extinction as something that occurs because of an external event: a meteor wipes out the dinosaurs, humans hunt something to non-existence. But a species can easily, logically, rationally destroy itself.

In the 1940s Price worked on the Manhattan Project, studying the chemical properties of plutonium. He was later given a job by the Galton Laboratory at University College, London when he walked in off the street with no references and no appointment, and told them he understood the evolutionary basis of altruism. They hired him that same day. He struggled with depression. He was a scathingly militant atheist—like Dawkins—until 1970, when he found God. He felt that he'd been divinely appointed to discover the Price equation, but he was also troubled by the moral implications of the evolutionary theory he'd helped develop, and the nihilistic worldview it pointed towards.

Political scientists have this very useful term: 'the tragedy of the commons'. A commons is a large pool of shared utility that many agents have access to. If you're a group of humans it might be a forest you can cut down for firewood, or a lake filled with fish, or the atmosphere and the oceans that absorb your greenhouse gas emissions. If you're a non-human predator, such as a Canada lynx, the commons is the number of snowshoe hares available for consumption. If you're a single cell in an animal, the commons are all the energy and nutrients available in the organism.

Competition for the commons is a classic prisoner's dilemma. Rational self-interest means you should try to outcompete all of your rivals to get as much utility from the commons as you can, and it's rational for them to do the same. So you might cut down all the wood, or catch all the fish, or eat all the hares on the snow tundra, or turn into a cancer cell and copy yourself as many times as possible, growing a tumour that diverts utility from the rest of the body and into your own self-replication. The tragedy is that if everyone follows their rational self-interest then the commons is depleted and everyone/everything dies. You can avert the tragedy by forming temporary alliances and coalitions, but the nature of the replicators is that they're always blindly iterating through genetic space, looking for ways to outcompete their rivals and maximise their own utility. And if they don't do this, their rivals will.

Richard Dawkins, writing as an evangelical atheist, believed that the problems of the world are due to a surplus of religious faith and a deficit of rationalism. But *The Selfish Gene*, written by Dawkins the biologist, shows that most of the hard problems of the world are due to replicators following rational strategies. If you're a baby bird in a nest and everyone else is chirping, it's rational to chirp louder. If you're a cell in a tumour and every other cell is rapidly proliferating, it's rational for you to do so too. You can 'choose' not to do those things, but then you'll simply get wiped out and replaced by replicating agents that chose differently. None of these agents are evil, but they are trapped in stable strategies that compel them to act in ways that are indistinguishable from evil.

In 1973, George Price became what effective altruists refer to as an extreme altruist. He devoted his entire life to helping strangers, even though his own theories suggested this form of altruism was irrational. He gave away his clothes and food and money; he invited many of the homeless people he encountered in central London to live with him in his rented apartment, which became so crowded he sometimes slept in his lab. He lost his job. Eventually his lease ended and he became homeless himself, drifting from one squatters' flat to another. At the same time, his collaborative papers with Maynard Smith were being published in the world's most prestigious science journals. Eventually he found work as a cleaner at a bank, but soon killed himself in an abandoned house scheduled for demolition.

*

I return to my kuti to change for lunch and this is when I learn I've forgotten to pack clean socks. This is really bad news. The main things you do in the monastery are work hard, get sweaty, walk along damp muddy paths and get wet feet, and sit in the meditation hall with no shoes on in close proximity to other people. I'm here for three more days and my only pair of socks already smells bad.

The first time I stayed here I forgot to bring a towel, and when I told one of the lay residents, assuming there was a large cupboard filled with spare towels I could use, they shrugged and suggested I take a flannel from the laundry and dry myself with that. And I did, and it was a miserable experience. Nobody here is going to lend me socks. The monks go barefoot all the time and they'll probably tell me to do the same. I walk back down the path, my socks squelching, trying to think of a solution. It's lunchtime, so I'm heading for the kitchen for the only substantial meal of the day.

The monastery exists to provide training and residence for the monks and to function as a religious centre for the wider Buddhist community. Almost every day a group of Buddhists in the region come here to cook the main meal of the day. They're usually South or South East Asian: Thai, Sri Lankan, Vietnamese, Cambodian, Laotian, and they're usually celebrating the birth of a child, or a birthday or wedding, or mourning the death of a relative. They offer up food to the monks in exchange for a blessing. And the food is phenomenal. It's served up in a large buffet. The protocol is that the monks always serve themselves first. They ladle the food into their large copper begging bowls, return upstairs and sit on cushions in the meeting hall above the kitchen. Once they're seated, the rest of us can serve ourselves.

I pile my plate high with rice and curry and chapatis and sit in the glass hall on the ground floor. The kōwhai tree opposite is filled with tūī, more than I've ever seen in a single tree before, a kaleidoscope of swaying branches and beating black wings. There must be at least twenty or thirty of the birds.

'That's unusual,' one of the older Sri Lankan visitors, a white-haired man in a suit and tie comments to the group. 'Tūī are usually quite solitary.'

'It's spring,' one of the younger women explains. 'It means they're going to have a lot more tūī.'

One of my duties is to help with the dishes, and because this is an enormous feast there are enormous piles of them. I'm strapping on an apron and filling the sinks with water when B comes and taps my shoulder. 'I'll do that,' he says. 'Ajahn is waiting to talk to you in the meeting room upstairs.'

*

Many people read *The Selfish Gene* and are distressed by its worldview, and some of them write letters to Richard Dawkins. In his memoir, *Unweaving the Rainbow: Science, Delusion and the Appetite for Wonder*, Dawkins publishes extracts from correspondents who've read his book and are so upset by it they can't eat, or sleep; they're spiralling into depression. Many of them wish they could unread it.

Dawkins is baffled by all of this. His book is true, isn't it? And he's not saying that humans are selfish, or that we're utterly controlled by our genes. All his examples are drawn from non-human animals. Other species might be disposable slaves for the replicators, but humans are obviously exceptional.

It's true that the case studies in *The Selfish Gene* are non-human: fish, birds, insects. There's a passage describing male butterflies fighting over patches of sunlight which they use to attract mates that has, for me, forever disenchanted the sight of butterflies fluttering in sunbeams. But most of the book talks about abstract behaviour, and it feels like Dawkins is talking about humans. He refers to mothers and fathers and grandmothers and children. Aggression and cooperation and deception. Altruism, territoriality. Love. All recognisably human behaviour, and all of it, the book reveals, attributable to the logic of replicators competing in strategic games.

When I first read *The Selfish Gene* I was troubled by it and enormously relieved by Dawkins' conclusions in his final chapter. Humans, Dawkins declares, make our own choices. We do this due to our superior access to reason and the imagination. We invented contraceptives, didn't we? This thwarts the will of the replicators, doesn't it? But, rereading the book, I think that the people who responded to it with insomnia and breakdowns were more perceptive than I was, and that they understood Dawkins' book better than he did.

We can invent and use contraception and thus thwart the will of the genes, which removes genes disposed towards this behaviour from the pool. But in making such a choice, are we *really* choosing, or are we just one of the many paths through genetic space that lead nowhere? Another evolutionarily stable strategy that leads to extinction?

We have reason and imagination, but our use of these

facilities is downstream from our desires, and our desires are downstream from the replicators. The mall I ate at yesterday was constructed using reason and imagination, and everything inside it—the food court, the shops, the theatres, the donut stand—was built to interact with the dopaminergic reward pathways in my brain, which was designed by the replicators. All of our wants are bounded by them.

*

'What was I like as a teenager?' Ajahn Kusalo considers the question, then replies, 'I was punk before punk was punk.'

'What does that mean?'

'It means I wore military clothes. Chains. Things like that.'

'So you dressed like a punk.'

'No.' He holds up a correcting finger. 'The punks dressed like me.'

The meeting room is carpeted, with white plaster walls on three sides. The fourth wall is glass, looking out over the courtyard and trees. There's a shrine at the far end with a Buddha statue surrounded by fresh flowers. The Abbot sits on a meditation cushion just to the side of the shrine, dressed in his brown robes, drinking tea from a china tea set. I sit on a brown circular cushion on the floor before him.

I ask, 'Can you tell me about the commune?'

'What commune?'

'The last time I was here you mentioned founding a commune. On Great Barrier Island.'

He nods. 'I was young and looking for an alternative. A way out of society.'

'What was it called?'

The Abbot hesitates. He looks at my notebook and narrows his eyes and asks, 'You said you wanted to talk about Buddhism and monasticism. What does any of this have to do with that?'

'Because this monastery is a community that works,' I reply. 'There are lots of people out there looking for alternatives, or a way out of society, and some of them found communes. But most communes fail. If you read the sociology literature on alternate societies, the ones that succeed tend to be religious. So I'm curious to know how your commune failed.'

The Abbot sips his tea. I wonder if our conversation is already over. Then he says, 'That particular commune failed because it succeeded. At the start it was very communal. And that's because it was hard, and we needed each other, and you always get unity through adversity. Someone needed to borrow my chainsaw. I needed to borrow their boat. So there was a mutual interdependence. But there was no spiritual core. As people get wealthier'—he points at me—'you don't need my chainsaw anymore. You can just hire a guy to do your chainsawing. Soon nobody needs each other. There's no shared value system because there's no spiritual dimension. No sense of the transcendent. Pretty soon you're not a commune anymore, you're just a group of people living separately on the same patch of land, with all the tensions that brings if there's nothing to keep you together.'

'What did you do after the commune?'

'I tried other communes. Other alternatives.' He laughs. 'There were a lot of strange spiritual movements around in the 1980s. Lots of derivations of Buddhism. Eventually I wound up in West Australia with my wife and son. We were heading for Asia but we ran out of money. So I looked in the phonebook under "B" for Buddhism, dialled the number and a monk answered. And that's how I became a Buddhist.'

'Did you get to Asia?'

'Eventually. I stayed in Perth for a while. Set up a factory there. Made cabinetry. I wound up with a qualification as a quantity surveyor. Then I came back here, solo parented for five years. My son's in the tech industry now. Doesn't really care about Buddhism. When he was old enough to look after himself I came here.'

'How long have you been a monk?'

'Twenty-eight years.'

'Have you ever met an enlightened being?'

'People ask me that sometimes.' He shrugs indifferently. 'If I say yes, what does it mean, and if I say no, what does that mean? Is the promise of enlightenment a marketing technique for spiritual movements? Of course. Some people get the idea that enlightenment is a box they can tick, or a form of power they can obtain, that they can use to control and exploit. But real transcendence goes in exactly the opposite direction. Other people want to believe there are heroes in the world who can solve all their problems. Like Superman, or John Wick.' His eyes narrow again. 'What are you smiling at? You think just because I live in a monastery I don't know about John Wick? And what's the other one they all love?' He thinks for a moment. Closes his eyes then opens them. 'Riddick.'

I'm tempted to ask the Abbot about his popular culture diet, but that might take the conversation down a path I can't get back from, so instead I say, 'This takes us back to the idea of communities and value systems. If you want to keep a community together, it's very useful to be able to say: the person who founded our community achieved enlightenment. They've seen the hidden true nature of existence, and based on their superior knowledge they've decreed that this is how we should live and these are the rules we have to follow, and the leaders of the community have privileged access to the same truths.'

'It does keep people tidy,' the Abbot concedes. 'Keeps them all lined up. To be part of a monastic community is to acquiesce to leadership. I often say: this monastery is a democratic dictatorship. I'm the dictator and everyone else is part of the democracy. And that's where the danger lies, of course. You get the mixing of church and state. Corruption. Abuse. That's the function of the Vinaya—the monastic code of ethics. It constrains the rulers. Celibacy, poverty and so on. And the ruler cannot change the rules. If they do they're no longer the ruler.'

'Does the system work?'

'Obviously there are failures. One of the oldest rules is that you can't charge money for teaching the dharma. Well, there's an order of monks in Thailand that sells real estate in one of the heavenly realms. If you pay them enough, you can buy a house with a pool in heaven. The same thing happens in the west. Prosperity gospels. TV evangelists. People think that they've worked hard so they deserve the things they want. They don't understand that the wanting never ends.'

'It's like a loop.'

'Exactly. I used to be very evangelical about Buddhism. I thought, "People need to know that we're all caught in a trap, this endless loop, and there's a way out. We can be free." But most people just want to be happy. They don't want to be free. And that's okay.'

'Aren't freedom and happiness . . . connected?'

'Are they? Freedom is a complicated thing. Most people are somewhat friendly towards Buddhism. It's palatable. We've never had a holy war. We've got the Dalai Lama. Most people will go with most of the five precepts.' He ticks them off on his fingers. 'Don't harm anyone. Don't steal anything. Don't tell lies. Don't be unfaithful. Some people have a problem with the fifth precept: sobriety. What's wrong with a few beers? Well, nothing. Unless you're an alcoholic, in which case giving you the freedom to drink takes away your freedom not to drink. If you're an alcoholic you can't choose. And most of us are alcoholics in some way. All of us have desires that compel us, and our society is very very good at manufacturing new desires. New drugs. Games people can't stop playing. Smartphones we can't stop using. And all of that behaviour is monetised. Why is YouTube free? Because Google owns it, and they want to commodify your compulsions. Why is GitHub free? Because Microsoft owns it.'

'How do you know about GitHub?' I'm genuinely intrigued. GitHub is a software development platform. I use it at work all the time, but I can't quite imagine how a Buddhist monk would stumble across it.

'I'm rebuilding the monastery's website,' he explains. 'In JavaScript. And I use GitHub as a code repository. Now, code,' he continues, 'is a useful way to think about meditation and freedom. I'm still learning to programme and that means I can only use the language the way it's designed to be used. If something goes wrong I don't know how to fix it. But once I'm an expert, once I understand how the language works under the hood, then I can do the things I want. Then I'm free. And that's the purpose of meditation. You're learning about how the mind really works and that opens up a very radical form of freedom. I've just been on self-retreat. I only ate every two days. I didn't have to do all that eating and chewing and excreting, and I felt very free. When you're out in the world you're free to eat whatever you want whenever you want it.' I glance down at my belly, involuntarily. It pokes out between my T-shirt and sweatpants. He asks, 'Do you feel free?'

*

I have a plan to wash and dry my socks.

Washing them is easy. I can just rinse them with hot water and dishwashing liquid in the bathroom sink, and wring them out a few times. Drying them is hard. It's pouring with rain. There's a small laundry room in the main building, but no dryer. I might be able to dry them in the oven, in the kitchen, but this could go wrong in several obvious ways. And then I remember the library. It's heated to keep the books warm. I'll wash my socks and dry them on the library heater. I hum a triumphant little tune to myself, fetch the detergent, wash my socks and then emerge from the men's bathroom barefoot to find that the key to the library—which was there, like, two minutes ago—has gone.

Carrying my wet socks, I walk across the sharp gravel stones to the library. The lights are out. The door is locked. There's no one there. I walk back across the stones to the main building. It's early afternoon. There's no one around. It's raining again. My feet are cold. My socks are sodden and cold in my hands. I can't even walk back to my kuti. I came out of my conversation with the Abbot with a deep sense of clarity and purpose, but this feels like a very low point on my spiritual path.

I decide to sit in the meditation hall and meditate, because that's what the Buddha would do in my situation. But I can't concentrate; I'm too distracted by my cold feet and frustrated plans. After about half an hour I get up and go outside, stand at the top of the steps leading down to the courtyard and stare at the rain with my hands in the pockets of my sweatpants, absently running my thumb along the ridges of the key in my left pocket. I do this for at least two minutes before I realise that the key in my pocket is the library key. I must have picked it up earlier.

The socks are cotton. Medium thickness. Orange. They'll

take some time to dry. I lay them out on top of the heater, position my frozen feet in front of it and take Heidegger's *Introduction to Metaphysics* down from the shelf, and spend the afternoon reading it as the rain comes down.

Introduction to Metaphysics, first published in 1953, is seen as a rather unsavoury book in philosophical circles. And the last time I stayed here the Abbot made it clear that the library should be used for studying Theravada Buddhism. So I shouldn't be reading western philosophy at all. But I keep going back to Heidegger in much the same way a teenager who grew up in a Christian home might listen to satanic metal. Heidegger is the great enemy of reason. His critique is, in some ways, rather Buddhist, and some commentators believe he was influenced by Schopenhauer, who was the first major philosopher in the western tradition to read Buddhist and Hindu texts in translation.

Bertrand Russell once declared that 'what science cannot discover, humans cannot know'. Heidegger replies that we cannot accept this state of affairs, because there are simply too many vital questions that science cannot answer, and the world that science reveals is too impoverished for us to live in.

If you ask a meteorologist why it's raining, they'll give you an answer describing weather patterns and chaotic systems. If you ask a chemist where these things come from, they'll tell you about water vapour and gas laws. Physicists can explain these phenomena in terms of elementary particles and fundamental forces. But we can't go back any further than that. We've hit the wall in terms of scientific explanations for the rain. And even if some new explanation or discipline explains the existence of particles and laws, that just pushes the problem back. There must be some deeper explanation beyond that explanation, and another beyond that. Looking for ultimate rational explanations in any direction always throws us into an infinite loop.

And it's the same with other deep philosophical problems. What is the causal explanation for the beginning of time? What—to ask Heidegger's favourite question—is Being? Why is there something rather than nothing? Why are we aware of the world instead of just part of it, like all the other matter we see around us? How should we live?

So Heidegger asks: is reason really the only tool that we have for knowing things about the world? Advocates for reason believe that science is objective and impartial; that they are seeing the world neutrally. One of Heidegger's aims in *Introduction to Metaphysics* is to 'deconstruct' rationalism, that is, to show that the scientific viewpoint, which sees itself as natural and impartial, is a very artificial construct, the product of two and a half thousand years of cultural and philosophical and linguistic development, and that its viewpoint of the world is very constrained. It cannot see many things, but it cannot see that it cannot see them. Rationalism is one path through the forest of existence; one route through the vector states of conceptual space, and it leads to some clearings, some ways of unconcealing the world, but it leaves much of existence dark.

Heidegger believes that there are other paths, and that it is urgent we explore them, because the path we are currently on—the path of rational modernity—has arrived at a dead end. The logical destination of modernity is what Heidegger calls 'machination'. He's referring not just to industrial machines, but rather to an understanding of the natural world in which everything is a machine. It's a *Selfish Gene* view of existence, basically, in which we're all temporary aggregations of particles competing for utility—'a revelation of beings as a whole as exploitable and manipulable objects', as he puts it. Rationalism locks us into a 'mathematisation of the world', which strips everything of meaning or purpose other than as available utility for rational self-interested agents to satisfy their subjective desires. Everything is a resource—natural resources, human resources, virtual resources. All is raw material to be acquired and processed.

Heidegger felt that the path of reason was probably an apocalyptic one: that it would end either in wars that annihilated our species or runaway resource consumption leading to ecological collapse. But sometimes he offered up an alternative nightmare scenario, a future in which:

> The world shines in the radiance of advances, advantages and material goods, where human rights are respected [. . .] and where, above all, there is a guaranteed supply that constantly satisfies an undisturbed comfort, so that everything can be overseen and everything remains calculable and manageable in terms of utility.

Me at the mall, basically. From Heidegger's perspective, Larkin's long slide 'to happiness, endlessly', becomes something monstrous. And he isn't just critiquing consumerism or capitalism here. He sees socialism and communism as indistinguishable from capitalism: they're all incarnations of modernity, materialist ideologies trying to deliver utopias which are actually technological prisons, dopaminergic traps in which we live impoverished, pointless lives but don't know it because we're so comfortable.

How do you escape the trap? Rationalism and materialism give us so much power over the world. They're a stable strategy, resistant to invasion, a loop you can't get out of. Heidegger's ambition was to find philosophical alternatives to modernity. But he knew that philosophy alone wasn't enough. You also needed cultural and political alternatives. That's one of the reasons he joined the Nazi Party when it rose to power in Germany in the early 1930s.

*

Heidegger is hard to read when you're tired. And I haven't slept well in a long time. I fall asleep in the library and am almost late for the evening puja. We start with the chanting, and I'm getting the hang of the Pali pronunciation so this goes rather well. But I spend most of the meditation period in a state of dullness. My mind is blurry, unfocused, drifting. This is not unpleasant: I feel warm. I see hypnagogic colours and patterns on the back of my eyelids. I float through a sequence of abstract, dreamlike thoughts. Eventually I doze off then wake myself with a ragged, bestial snore to find myself pitching forward on my meditation stool, about to fall face down onto the floor. I jolt upright.

It takes me a long time to walk back to my kuti. It's raining. I stop to rest at the top of an incline, and on a whim I shine the beam of my torch up towards the sky, transforming the rain into threads of white light. I have a brief Buddha-mixed-with-Heidegger vision of humans as sentient rain, countless billions of us pouring into existence out of nowhere, briefly lit then falling back into darkness.

I wake early. It's my third day at the monastery, and I sit up in my sleeping bag and look out at the mist and feel a pleasant lack of hunger. I think about the Abbot's comments on freedom. When I'm out in the world, living my everyday life, I feel relieved that I'm not accountable to a church, or state, or Ajahn Kusalo to tell me what I can and cannot eat.

But now that I'm here, spending a few days outside my own life, the freedom to eat uncontrollably until I die of cancer or heart disease does seem like a strange form of freedom.

I think about the Abbot's comment: 'Freedom is a complicated thing.' I think about the most famous idea in *The Selfish Gene*, which isn't even about genes. Towards the end of the book Dawkins introduces one of his most controversial theories: memes. These are cultural replicators: the non-physical equivalent of genes. Memes are languages, songs, gestures, rituals, the theories of Martin Heidegger; anything that can travel from one mind to another. Like genes, memes can replicate, mutate and respond to selective pressure. They're living things, Dawkins argues, in the very literal sense, and from his perspective, religions are viral memes: obey me in life and make as many copies of me as you can and you'll be rewarded after death. They're parasitic, they infect the mind. They function as tools of oppression, causing terrible bloodshed when they clash with their religious or ideological memetic rivals.

At the beginning of the work period, B and I stand in the courtyard awaiting orders. There are baskets of flowers everywhere: lilies, succulents, ferns, roses. The monks are hanging up banners of prayer flags.

I've been wondering how long you have to meditate to achieve the insights into the nature of mind that Ajahn Kusalo talked about, so I ask B if he's had any insight experiences. He gives me a wary glance and replies, 'I've learned that it's not a good idea to have deep and meaningful conversations in monasteries.'

'Isn't that the only kind of conversation we're allowed to have here?'

'People have insights and experiences,' he replies, 'but they interpret them in different ways. If you try to discuss them everything gets confused. I think the best thing is to keep the conversations superficial and work the deep stuff out for yourself.'

'Huh.'

He points at the flags. 'Did you know that the Buddhist flag was designed by an admiral in the US Navy?'

'I did not.' I consider the flag. It has bright multicoloured vertical and horizontal stripes. 'Do the stripes represent, like, wisdom and compassion . . . ?'

'Yeah. I'm pretty sure white is purity.'

'Makes sense. Orange?'

'I think orange is wisdom.'

'Red?'

'I don't know about red.'

We keep looking at the flags, trying to figure out what the colours mean, then jump in alarm when Ajahn Kusalo materialises out of a shadowy corner of the courtyard.

'Danyl. B. Follow me.' He sweeps past, leading us up a flight of concrete steps. 'It's time for you to be initiated into the esoteric secrets of the monastery.'

'What secrets?' B sounds wary. 'What initiation?'

'Don't worry. All it'll require is a small blood sacrifice.'

The Abbot's voice is light. I think he's probably joking, but B has known him longer than I have, and isn't so sure. He asks, 'Blood from who?'

'From you.' The Abbot leads us to a stone plinth with a Buddha statue mounted atop it. 'Kneel down,' he instructs and we obey, moderately terrified. 'This Buddha can be detached from the plinth.' He instructs us in the rather elaborate hidden mechanism for doing this. 'Like so. And when it's free I want you to carry it down to the wooden table in the centre of the courtyard. It is extremely heavy, so be careful. Lift with your knees.'

We stand once we've released the statue, and I get ready to lift when B taps my shoulder and asks, 'Did you see me hit my head?' I look over at him. There's a cut above his right eyebrow and he's bleeding.

'Did you just do that?'

'Yeah. I hit my forehead on the base.' He touches his hand to the wound and it comes away with quite a lot of blood. 'Whoa.'

'Head wounds bleed a lot,' I say. 'You'll need a bandage.'

We walk back down the stairs, behind the Abbot. 'Damn,' B complains. 'You said there'd be a blood sacrifice. You called it.'

Ajahn Kusalo does not reply. Nor does he appear displeased by this sequence of events. When we reach the bottom of the stairs the other monks see the blood running down the side of B's face and hurry over. 'What happened?'

The Abbot replies, 'The Buddha bit him.'

*

There's an apocryphal story about Heidegger delivering an earlier lecture on metaphysics entitled 'What is Metaphysics?' At the end of the lecture, so the story goes, there was a deep silence, eventually broken by a lone voice querying, 'Professor Heidegger? What is metaphysics?' to which Heidegger replied, 'Good question.'

Heidegger is famously opaque. Hannah Arendt called him 'the secret king of thought', and he's often cited as the most influential philosopher of the twentieth century, but he doesn't make it easy for us. The challenge in understanding

Heidegger is that he doesn't want to be understood, at least not in ways that can be easily explained, because he thinks that the language we use and the framework we think with are part of the problem with the world. His project is not to prove or disprove things, or to communicate ideas via language, or any of the usual concerns of philosophers, but rather to change the type of ideas that we can have and the language that we think them with.

What is metaphysics? It is all the problems that physics and the other sciences cannot solve. Causality, consciousness, being, time. Heidegger's assertion is that the modern scientific worldview is built on assumptions that it cannot explain, or can never prove. His goal as a philosopher is to build a radically different worldview: a new way of thinking and speaking and relating to existence.

We see ourselves as individuals who occupy bodies that move around in space. We experience the world subjectively, and are closed off from each other and the rest of existence. Heidegger wants us to understand ourselves differently. Instead of experiencing the world as subjects interacting with external objects, he portrays us as 'the world opening up to itself'. Instead of impartial rational observers, we are historical constructs, built from language and culture. Instead of individuals, we co-exist with the members of our community in a web of mutual cooperation, understanding and responsibility. If we reject modernity and adopt this alternative way of being in the world we can, he claims, lead more authentic and meaningful lives.

Heidegger's most famous book is *Being and Time*, and these subjects are the basis for his conceptual system. He's confident that no physicist or psychologist will ever dismantle his assertions about either of them. Unlike Christianity, say, which made falsifiable assertions about the creation and nature of the world, Heidegger's system is designed to be immune to rational attacks.

Introduction to Metaphysics was first delivered as a lecture series at the University of Freiburg in 1935, about two years after Heidegger became a Nazi and about one year after his attempt to establish himself as the lead philosopher of the National Socialist movement failed. This failure was partly due to his political ineptitude, partly because rival intellectuals in the Nazi movement announced that Heidegger's abstract and difficult ideas had little or nothing to do with their—or anyone else's—conception of fascism. Even though the lectures were delivered after his failed entry into politics, they still praise 'the inner truth and greatness' of National Socialism.

When the *Introduction* was published, after the war, Heidegger insisted that it contained a secret critique of Nazism, if you read it in just the right way. But he never publicly apologised for being a Nazi. If anyone should apologise to anyone, he commented to a colleague, Hitler should be brought back to life to apologise to Heidegger. The Führer's version of National Socialism was, he felt, just another nightmarish incarnation of modernity. With its failure there were now no alternatives to materialism, machination, the death of Being. There was no hope. In 1966 Heidegger agreed to an interview with *Der Spiegel* on the condition that it would only be published posthumously. In it he declared, bitterly, 'Only a god can save us.'

Lunch is another gigantic buffet. Vietnamese. Amazing. After we've washed the dishes I try to strike up a friendly conversation with S, who greeted me on my first day and runs the kitchen.

'So, you're from Malaysia?'

'Malaysia. Yes.'

'How long have you lived in New Zealand?'

Pause. 'Are you looking for some work to do?'

'Not really. I mean . . . I'm happy to help, if you want. Although I did work this morning. I was just asking—'

'There's a broom in the carport. You can sweep the paths around the library.'

There are a lot of red and pink camellia blossoms on the paths around the library and it takes me a long time to sweep them all up. Afterwards I wash my socks and spend the remainder of the afternoon drying them on the library heater, dutifully reading a collection of the sayings of Ajahn Chah, the founder of the Forest Monastery tradition.

The Forest Tradition is a new monastic order. But it's very traditional and very conservative. Like the Christian monastic tradition, Buddhism tends to follow historical cycles. Monasteries are founded by spiritual leaders who renounce the world and seek a more contemplative life. They draw followers to them because every society is filled with lots of people who don't want to live in it. Over time, the monasteries transform into powerful, rather secular, rather corrupt institutions, and eventually there's a reformation and another return to austerity and spirituality.

The Forest Tradition was a reaction to the 'luxurious and uncontemplative' form of monasticism practised in Thailand in the early twentieth century, in which very few of the Buddha's monastic codes were observed and meditation was seen as a bizarre and suspicious practice that might expose the meditator to possession by evil spirits. Ajahn Chah was born in 1918. He lived as a mendicant monk for a while, rising to become the Forest Tradition's spiritual leader, and founded his first monastery in a grove amidst a dense forest 'known as a place for cobras, tigers and ghosts'. In the 1960s he began training westerners and establishing monasteries in the west, and by the early twenty-first century there were about three hundred Forest Tradition monasteries around the world.

Before the evening puja ceremony I speak with one of the Thai monks at Bodhinyanarama. He's slender and small, wears very large, thick eyeglasses that cover about half his face, and radiates an aura of wisdom and humour. He is generally very Dalai-Lama-like. We chat for a while about the monastery, the dharma, the innate emptiness of everything.

The first time I stayed here, one of the long-term guests told me that this monk was one of the wisest they'd met, and that I should ask him for meditation advice. So I explain to the monk that I've been meditating for about two years, mainly concentration meditation, and ask if I should widen my practice to include more insight meditation. And he replies, 'No.'

'No? Shouldn't I be trying to perceive the true nature of existence?'

'First you need a stable mind.'

'I feel pretty stable. Don't I seem stable?'

He says, as kindly as possible, 'No.'

I open my mouth to argue my case, then remember that it's been about two weeks since I slept properly, that I had a strange apocalyptic vision in the mall three days ago, and that last night I spent about ten minutes shining my torch up into the rain and thinking about tranquillity and ruin. I close my mouth again.

He tells me, 'Practise concentration until the mind is stable.'

'What should I do when my mind is stable?'

'If I tell you now I'll just confuse you. But when the mind is stable you'll know what to do without me telling you.'

*

In the mid-1960s, the western philosophical tradition realised it had split into two distinct streams. There was the analytic school, which tends to be logical and rational and scientific, and the continental tradition, which exists outside of, and critiques, the analytics. (Everyone agrees that the names for the traditions are terrible and make no sense, and that both categories are almost impossible to define, but everyone uses them anyway.)

The analytics respond to Heidegger in a number of ways. First: does he even make any sense? When Heidegger claims, for example, that 'the nothing nothings', is he advancing a philosophical argument, or is he forming sentences that are literally meaningless and merely pretending that they have depth? If 'nothing' is the absence of anything, how can 'the nothing' do anything, and what could the 'nothings' that nothing is allegedly doing consist of?

Heidegger's defenders reply that Heidegger is trying to express existential truths outside the narrow bounds of rationalism, so of course you can show that his statements are non-rational. That's the whole point of his project. But, his critics reply, what criteria do we use to judge the validity of such 'non-rational truths'? Can anyone say literally anything and insist that it is a non-rational truth, and if not, why not? Maybe not everyone, continental philosophers might reply, can say anything. But we often identify great poetry or great art as expressing a profound emotional truth. When Yeats tells us: 'Like a long-legged fly upon the stream / His mind moves upon silence', we respond to these words, at least I do, even though they are vulnerable to the same logical critique as Carnap's attack on Heidegger ('How can the mind move upon silence?'). Heidegger thought philosophy should be more like poetry; his critics wanted it to be more like math.

Secondly, Heidegger sees modernity as 'the death of Being', but the vast majority of people born prior to modernity endured lives of incredible drudgery and suffering. They had no vaccines, antibiotics or anaesthetics. About a quarter of all infants died before they were a year old. Overall, child mortality rates were about 50 per cent. Average life expectancy was about thirty years. Prior to industrialisation most people worked on farms their whole lives, until they died of famine or disease, or in childbirth, or by violence. How awake to the mystery of Being were the people living under these conditions? How terrible is rationalism if it can relieve such unimaginable suffering, and what have any of these 'other ways of being in the world' accomplished that can compare with the invention of antibiotics?

Finally, we can ask: where did Heidegger's alternative path through the forest of existence take him? Did it lead to a more spiritually pure and authentic life? It did not. It led to the Nazi Party, and many of Heidegger's intellectual heirs became apologists for Stalin or other forms of totalitarian Communism.

So it's easy for the Analytics to dismiss Heidegger. 'A bad man,' the analytic philosopher Gilbert Ryle reputedly said of him, 'must be a bad philosopher.' Karl Popper called Heidegger a devil and beseeched the world of philosophy 'to unite and never again mention him'. Rudolf Carnap—one of the most influential thinkers of the analytic school—dismissed metaphysicians like Heidegger as 'musicians without musical ability'.

But many of Heidegger's most brilliant students were Jewish. They thought he was a great philosopher who had—rather obviously—lost his way, but that his ideas were too important to ignore. Leo Strauss, the most influential conservative intellectual of the twentieth century, who studied under Heidegger at Freiberg before fleeing the Nazis, first to London then the United States, was one of them.

Strauss was primarily a political thinker. Like many post-war intellectuals he was concerned with the problem of building a good society. Why did catastrophes like Nazi Germany and Soviet Russia occur? How could you avoid them? And what obligations did intellectuals and philosophers have towards the societies they lived in? Strauss would have been murdered if his academic career hadn't allowed him to flee Germany, and Heidegger—that nation's most brilliant thinker—would have quietly approved. Philosophers and other intellectuals needed to do better.

Strauss believed that every society needs a foundation: a story and accompanying moral code that validates the authority of the state while also protecting the citizens from the depredations of their rulers. And he believed that this foundation needed to be religious in nature: that Plato's Noble Lie was the only basis for a sustainable society. If the rules were sacred, then the rulers could not breach or change them without invalidating their right to rule. Meanwhile, the faith allowed the rest of society to live together and believe that their lives were meaningful.

Modernity was able to discredit almost all of those religious systems. It revealed that the Noble Lies were just lies. But it wasn't able to replace religious morality with anything meaningful. Rationalism can reveal that there is no objective morality and no meaning to existence, Strauss felt, but any society which believes this will fail. The reason rulers like Hitler and Stalin appeared, Strauss believed, was that under conditions of rational modernity there was no longer any shared value system by which to reject them.

Strauss's proposed solution to this problem is that philosophers, and other sceptical intellectuals, must accept Heidegger's critique of reason. We live in a universe that is ultimately mysterious, and the questions most non-intellectuals want answers to—how we should live, why our lives matter, how we can live together—lie outside the boundaries of rational inquiry. Only revelation—religious visions and sacred laws—can speak to these questions. Or, at least, pretend to do so. Reason can disprove religious claims (unless you're cunning and base your system on metaphysical problems the way Heidegger did, or the subjective experience of an enlightened being, like the Buddhists). But only the moral systems of religious traditions can address the failures of reason.

So the two traditions—reason and revelation—exist in perpetual tension. But Strauss felt they needed each other. Reason reins in the excesses of faith, while faith reminds philosophers and scientists that they see less than they think they do, and that they are not merely rational self-interested individuals. They're members of a society, which they have obligations towards. And in return they gain the benefits of living in that society, even if they don't share its beliefs. It doesn't matter if the faith is true, Strauss taught. What matters is that it is seen to be true.

*

I wash the breakfast dishes, yet again, only this time I'm joined by R, the other white-robed monk in training. He's in his mid-twenties, did an engineering degree, suffered from acute depression, started meditating, wound up here. We talk about the similarities and differences between universities and monasteries.

'Universities used to be monastic,' R points out. 'In some

ways they still are. Some of my maths lecturers were very otherworldly. Like, more than most monks.'

'But monasteries are radically different alternatives to secular society,' I reply. 'If you want to live somewhere like this, somewhere that's meditative and non-materialistic and communal, you're not going to find that in academia. It's just another branch of the real world.'

He smiles. 'I think this is the real world.'

'It does feel like that when you're here.' I dump a bowl of dirty cutlery in the sink. 'I think a lot of people would prefer to live someplace like this, if they knew it was an option. And if it wasn't religious.'

'It has to be religious,' R replies. 'That's the whole point.'

'Yeah, that's the tricky part.'

It's my last day at the monastery. The festival starts at 11am, which is the same time my wife and daughter will pick me up outside the gates and take me to a family event. 'I can't get out of it,' I explain to the monks and lay residents. Everyone seems genuinely sorry for me that I have to leave early. But I'm relaxed about it. I miss my family and I don't like festivals.

Although, Kathina seems nicer than most. There's no PA system. No live bands. No food trucks with endless queues. The air does not reek of pot. More and more people arrive, mostly families—kids, teenagers, parents, grandparents. Everyone seems to know each other. Everyone brings food.

The monks from the other Buddhist temples and monasteries in the region arrive in minivans. Processions of monks in brown, red, orange and yellow robes pour out of the vans. B informs me that the colour of the robes depends on the pigments of dye from the vegetation in the different countries. The monks cross the courtyard, pressing their palms in greeting to everyone. The diplomats arrive in black SUVs driven by guys in black suits with black sunglasses. Everyone is dressed in their best clothes, except for me. I'm wearing trackpants and a dirty T-shirt because I've spent all morning washing dishes, sweeping paths and running extension cords through the cobwebbed rafters of the cloister.

The walls at the front of the meditation hall slide open and the large Buddha statue in the shrine now looks directly out into the cloister. When the ceremony begins everyone sits on cushions in the cloister or the hall, while the monks sit on a raised platform before the statue, facing the crowd. Ajahn Kusalo sits in the centre, chanting hymns of greeting in multiple languages.

I stand at the back. I haven't thought about eating all morning but now that my bags are packed, I've cleaned out my kuti and I'm about to leave, I realise I'm starving. And the trestle tables beside me are piled high with food. There are stacked silver dishes of curry, plates of breads, huge bowls of white and brown and coconut-scented rice. There are desserts, mounds of fruit, sliced mangos. There are cakes. And there are pastries, including mini chocolate eclairs filled with cream.

We're not supposed to eat until the monks have eaten. And that won't happen for a long time. After the opening chants, everyone will be given a paper plate which they'll pile with rice from the rice cookers, then they'll stand in a long line, offering rice to the monks, who will take some from each person. Then there will be more chanting. Then the monks will eat. Finally everyone else will eat. Lunch is hours away and I'll be long gone.

But everyone in the room has their back to me, except for the monks, who seem to have their eyes closed for this stage of the ceremony. After a struggle with my conscience, which lasts more than one second but less than three, I turn, take one of the mini chocolate eclairs and place it in my mouth. I think it tastes good, but I swallow it so quickly it barely registers on my taste buds. When I turn around again, Ajahn Kusalo's eyes are open and I have no doubt he saw me.

Time to leave. But then, just as I'm about to go, something odd happens. A jogger appears. He comes from around the side of the meditation hall and runs through the cloister, right through the vast space filled with monks and children and diplomats and security guards and men in suits and women in saris. I know where he's come from: one of the trails around the hill comes out behind the hall. Occasionally people who live in the area walk or run along it. But they normally do this when the cloister is empty, which is most of the time, not when it's teeming with people and the air reverberating with chants.

The jogger is in late middle age. He's white—almost the only white guy here other than the Abbot, a couple of other monks and myself. He's bald and dressed in short shorts and a tight T-shirt, and he's in terrific shape, lean and muscular. He looks like an ad for a promising longevity supplement. But as he runs through, no one else seems to notice him. No heads turn as he passes, and he seems weirdly indifferent to the sacred festival going on around him, doesn't even glance at the choir of deep-voiced monks intoning songs from the ancient past. I have this disconcerting sensation that I'm the only person who can see both the jogger and the crowd. And then he runs past me, smiling, and down the ramp and across the courtyard. I pick up my backpack and follow him. I feel a strange compulsion not to let him out of sight, so I break into a little jog myself, my backpack jostling on my back, my potbelly bouncing beneath my T-shirt. I chase him down the driveway and out through the gates, along the road to the intersection and into a different world.

Afterword

Every weekday I meet my daughter after school and we catch the bus home. The bus stop is on a busy street opposite a supermarket, and the bus is usually late. Today it has rained off and on for most of the day. The streets are wet; the air is filled with white noise. When we reach the bus stop, I sit, take out my cellphone and start the timer.

Sadie peers over at it. 'Whatcha doing?'

'Timing our bus.'

'Why?'

'You see the timetable?' I point at the digital display mounted on a pole and ask, 'How long till our bus arrives?'

She reads the display. 'Five minutes.'

'Ah! But how long till it really arrives?'

She gives me a wary look. 'Five minutes?'

'Or is it? My theory,' I explain, 'is that a minute in the bus timetable software is longer than a real minute. One minute might even be two minutes. But it's probably closer to ninety seconds. So when they say the bus is five minutes away it might be eight minutes until it actually arrives.'

She gasps. 'I'm eight!'

'Sure. So my plan is to time our bus every night this week and see if it's consistently later than the time on the display.'

'Why?'

'Because if it is, it proves they're using these things to lie to us. And by tricking us about how long we have to wait for the bus to arrive, they're stealing increments of our lives.'

'What's a increment?'

'A tiny part. See, they're taking these little bits of our time, slowly, individually, covertly, but when you add it up over a year, across all the passengers, it's huge. Entire lifetimes.'

Sadie breathes in sharply, comprehending. 'They're killing us.'

'Yes. Well, not quite. Kind of. Anyway, if I can prove they're misleading us I'll publish it in the media.'

'And then the bus drivers will go to jail.'

'Not the drivers. The people who run the company. And they won't go to jail.' I want Sadie to grow up with realistic expectations. 'Probably they'll say they're reviewing their systems.'

She nods, her eyes clear. 'And then they'll fix them.'

'Well, they won't do that either. They probably won't change anything.'

'Oh.' My project sounds meaningless to her, and, now that I've said it out loud, to me as well. She looks back at the timetable and says, 'Four minutes!' then asks, 'What is a minute?'

'A minute is sixty seconds.'

'What's a second?'

I always thought I'd be good at the scientific explanations part of being a dad. I know, for example, why the sky is blue. But none of my explanations ever work out the way I hope. When

Sadie asks me questions about animals or plants—'Why do we have five fingers?' 'Where do trees come from?'—I know too much to make my answers comprehensible. When I try to answer chemistry or physics questions ('What is electricity?', or the most recent example: 'Does water float?') I realise I know a lot less about those subjects than I thought I did.

'What is a second?' Time is hard to talk about. (Augustine: 'If no one asks me, I know what it is. If I wish to explain it to him who asks, I do not know.') I have a vague memory from undergraduate chemistry that time is linked to entropy, to the increase in a state of disorder within a system. To ruin. But I'm not sure I remember the details correctly, and even if I do, that seemed a little too much to explain to a mildly curious eight year old.

'A second is . . .' I look around, then point. 'Okay. Look at that office building. Imagine someone fell off the top.'

Sadie blinks at this thought and says brightly, 'They would die.'

'Yes. But imagine that the building was very high. Infinitely high. They'd fall but never reach the ground. They'd just keep falling and falling. That's one way to think about time. We can move around in space'—I wave my hands about and she flicks her eyes towards me then back to the building—'but time is something we fall through. And we measure our movement in hours and days and minutes and seconds. We're not moving through space, because we're sitting here, but we're always falling through time at the rate of one second per second. Does that make sense?'

She nods. 'And the seconds go on and on?'

'Yes.'

'Until we die?'

'Yes.'

I get nervous when Sadie asks me about death. Some people who meditate a lot experience what Buddhists call 'purifications'. These are memories, or purely emotional reactions that surge up into consciousness when the mind is free of distraction. The memories are often from childhood. They can be traumatic. Some people find them therapeutic, others intensely distressing.

I looked forward to this. Maybe I'd get purifications and some long-buried childhood trauma would explain my depression, and maybe even cure it. But when the memories came they were mostly from my adult life and mostly involved me being a bad person, dishonest or thoughtless or cruel, and then conveniently forgetting about it. It was traumatising, but not in the way I'd expected.

I do have a specific childhood memory that keeps coming back. I don't know if I buried it, so much as simply didn't think about it for thirty years. It's a memory of lying in bed late at night, unable to sleep because I was worried about dying. I'm about ten years old in the memory, a few years older than Sadie, and it's the mid-1980s, so my anxiety focuses on a dread of nuclear war, the fear that I might be incinerated in my sleep. The emotional tone of those memories is drenched in anxiety and depression, and I wonder if that's where some of my midlife sadness comes from. I worry that Sadie will go through something similar if she thinks about death too much.

She stares at me now, and seems to be thinking intensely about our conversation and I wonder how to redirect it, but then she says, 'Your beard is turning white.'

'I know. It makes me look dignified.'

'It looks like white string is growing out of your chin.'

*

I've spent some of the day at the library, writing one of the essays in this book and trying to read *Being and Time*. I've been trying to understand Heidegger's conception of time. He thought we had it wrong, just as we have everything wrong. We'd mathematicised time, broken it up into interchangeable increments: hours, minutes, seconds, and we saw ourselves as physical bodies occupying an endless series of homogenous now points strung out across eternity.

He thought it made more sense for us to conceive of ourselves as events, as beings that are fundamentally made of time. Instead of bodies we are made up of the past—of history, culture, language, and of the choices we can make in the present, and of the certain knowledge that our future is foreclosed by mortality. We are temporary openings in the darkness of existence, openings that are bound up with one another, and which lie stretched out between birth and death.

I think there's something to this. But what I also get from meditation is that, contra Heidegger, we are innately physical beings. Whenever I meditate while depressed or anxious— and I've learned that I'm always at least slightly anxious and/or slightly depressed, although generally in a low grade, background way that wouldn't be detectable if I weren't sitting silently and examining my own thoughts—I can sense the mood disorder, even after my thoughts have cleared. It presents as physical feelings of exhaustion, or tension, or both, a bath of hormones and neurotransmitters saturating my nervous system. Everything I think is drenched in it.

Heidegger wants us to choose paths through existence as we pass through time, but I'm not sure we can do this. Because we are physical beings trapped in the bodies of evolved animals, our freedom to choose is very narrow. I can't choose what to think or feel. I can't choose to sleep, or wake, or what I want to eat, or to forget something, or to remember something I know I've forgotten. Instead of choosing paths through time, I'm falling through it while experiencing the illusion of choice.

The only thing I can really choose is to pay attention to something, but only for a few seconds. That's the crack in the conditioned nature of things that meditation exploits; the leverage that seems to allow a small window of freedom through which we can start to control who we are and what we do. Although, when I asked a monk if awakening meant real choice and real freedom, they told me it meant the realisation that we never were free and never can be, and that this realisation is liberation. So there's that.

It's raining softly and the light is failing. It has been more than five minutes, and the timer on my phone is still running. The bus is still coming. The streets are wet and teeming, and as the rain comes down harder all of the noise softens and fades and the lights from the cars and streetlights fade into one another, running the colour of rain. The raindrops fall, slowly, and Sadie and I sit at the bus stop holding hands, slowly falling through time together.

Acknowledgements

Thanks to the teachers and staff at the Wangapeka Study and Retreat Centre. To the New Zealand Effective Altruists, who allowed me to attend and write about their retreat, especially Catherine Low and the other leaders of the movement who organised it all. I'm also indebted to the monks and lay stewards of the Bodhinyanarama Buddhist Monastery in Stokes Valley.

Thanks to Scott Hamilton, who encouraged me to read *Being and Time* and gave me a list of supplementary authors to unravel what any of it meant, and Matthew Hooton, who convinced me to read *Reasons and Persons*. It took me about six months to read and reread those two books, and they taught me more and made me think more than any of the dozens of more accessible books I might read in any given year.

I wrote some of these essays as part of my masters degree at Victoria University's International Institute of Modern Letters: thanks to Chris Price, who runs the non-fiction and poetry MA, and to my classmates, who read my hastily written drafts of the second and third essay, and pretended that they made sense.

Thanks again to the staff at Victoria University Press, especially Fergus Barrowman, who convinced me that a photo he took from his office window would make a great front cover, and Kirsten McDougall, who convinced us both that it would not. Ashleigh Young was my thesis supervisor and editor. She talked me out of most of my worst ideas, including my scheme to format the book with dense blocks of text separated by expanses of white space, which, looking back, made the essays look like lengthy menus but made sense to me somehow, at the time ('the form itself is meditative!').

And thanks again to Maggie and Sadie, to whom this book is dedicated.

Notes

Foreword

11 The political scientist Eitan Hersh calls this 'political hobbyism':
Eitan Hersh, 'College-Educated Voters Are Ruining Politics',
The Atlantic, 20 Jan. 2020. theatlantic.com/ideas/archive/2020/01/
political-hobbyists-are-ruining-politics/605212/

Arise and Pass Away

21 'In 2010, *Science* published a Harvard study': Matthew A. Killingsworth
and Daniel T. Gilbert, 'A Wandering Mind Is an Unhappy Mind',
Science 220, no. 6006 (12 Nov. 2010): 932. doi: 10.1126/science.1192439
25 'the mind becomes like a brightly lit room': Culadasa (John Yates),
with Matthew Immergut and Jeremy Graves, *The Mind Illuminated:
A Complete Meditation Guide* (Atria, 2015), 215. The full quotation
is: 'You begin this Stage with a more energized mind, so objects of
attention are clear and vivid. Peripheral awareness is also brighter and
more open. Just as turning up the light in a dark room illuminates
objects in the shadows, your heightened conscious power reveals
thoughts and sensations previously too subtle to detect.'
26 'We never see the world as our retina sees it': Stanislas Dehaene,
*Consciousness and the Brain: Deciphering How the Brain Codes Our
Thoughts* (Penguin, 2014), 60.
27 Yeats's phrase: 'Consume my heart away; sick with desire / And
fastened to a dying animal / It knows not what it is; and gather me
/ Into the artifice of eternity.' 'Sailing to Byzantium', *The Collected
Poems of W. B. Yeats*, edited by Richard J. Finneran (Wordsworth,
1994), 163.

33 'Quite secluded from sense pleasures, secluded from unwholesome states of mind . . .': The *Digha Nikaya* 2.77, quoted in Leigh Brasington, *Right Concentration: A Practical Guide to the Jhānas* (Shambhala Publications, 2015), 45.

39 'An illusion is not something that does not exist': Susan Blackmore, 'There Is No Stream of Consciousness', *Journal of Consciousness Studies* 9, no. 5–6 (May 2002), 17. susanblackmore.uk/articles/there-is-no-stream-of-consciousness/

40 'There's an infamous psychological study from 2014': Timothy D. Wilson, David A. Reinhard, Erin C. Westgate et al., 'Just Think: The Challenges of the Disengaged Mind', *Science* 345, no. 6192 (4 July 2014): 75–77. doi: 10.1126/science.1250830

50 'the biologist T.H Huxley took great delight in declaring that consciousness was an "epiphenomenon"': T.H. Huxley, 'On the Hypothesis that Animals are Automata, and its History', *Nature* 10 (3 Sept. 1874): 362–66. doi: 10.1038/010362a0

55 'Dreams seem to "prune redundancy and reduce complexity"': J.A. Hobson and K.J. Friston, 'Waking and Dreaming Consciousness: Neurobiological and Functional Considerations, *Progress of Neurobiology* 98, no.1 (July 2012): 82–98. doi: 10.1016/j.pneurobio.2012.05.003

60 'The meditation author and teacher Leigh Brasington theorises that the first jhana has something to do with distraction': Brasington, *Right Concentration*, 36–46.

The Child and the Open Sea

66 'Famine, Affluence and Morality' was first published in *Philosophy and Public Affairs* 1, no.3 (1972): 229–43. jstor.org/stable/2265052

69 'They quit their day jobs and founded GiveWell': Stephanie Strom, '2 Young Hedge Fund Veterans Stir Up the World of Philanthropy', *New York Times*, 20 Dec. 2017. nytimes.com/2007/12/20/us/20charity.html

72 'In 2009 the Oxford philosophers Toby Ord and William MacAskill founded Giving What We Can': 'Our History', Giving What We Can, accessed 19 Oct. 2020. givingwhatwecan.org/about-us/history/

— 'He cited donations to the blind': 'Taking Charity Seriously: Toby Ord Talk on Charity Effectiveness', *Less Wrong* (blog), April 2013. lesswrong.com/posts/iCa9JXAXAuCzuv3DT/taking-charity-seriously-toby-ord-talk-on-charity

73 'Effective altruism is about asking "How can I make the biggest difference I can?"': William MacAskill, *Doing Good Better* (Penguin, 2015), 11–12.

85 Spock as 'the naive archetype of rationality': Eliezer Yudkowsky, *Map and Territory* (*Rationality: From AI to Zombies Book One*), (Machine Intelligence Research Institute, 2018), 27.

88 '30% better than intelligence officers with access to actual classified information': 'So You Think You're Smarter Than a CIA Agent', Morning Edition, NPR, 2 April 2014. npr.org/sections/parallels/2014/04/02/297839429/-so-you-think-youre-smarter-than-a-cia-agent

— 'Tetlock calls them "superforecasters"': Philip Tetlock and Dan Gardner, *Superforecasting: The Art and Science of Prediction* (Penguin Random House, 2015).

93 'Is the truth depressing? Some may find it so': Derek Parfit, *Reasons and Persons* (Oxford University Press, 1984), 281.

96 'Imagine that you are creating a fabric of human destiny with the object of making men happy in the end': Fyodor Dostoevsky, *The Brothers Karamazov*, translated by Constance Garnett (Random House, 2012), 272.

97 Utility as 'that property in any object, whereby it tends to produce benefit, advantage, pleasure, good, or happiness': Jeremy Bentham, 'Chapter I: On the Principle of Utility', *An Introduction to the Principles of Morals and Legislation* (Clarendon Press, 1879; first published 1789), 2.

102 'In 2015 Daniel Kahneman told a *Guardian* journalist that the most dangerous form of heuristic bias is overconfidence': David Shariatmadari, 'Daniel Kahneman: "What would I eliminate if I had a magic wand? Overconfidence", *Guardian*, 18 July 2015. theguardian.com/books/2015/jul/18/daniel-kahneman-books-interview

109 'Stuart Russell likes to compare an improperly aligned AGI to the legend of King Midas': Robert Wiblin and Keiran Harris, 'The Flaws that Make Today's AI Architecture Unsafe and a New Approach That

Could Fix It', 80,000 Hours, 22 June 2020. 80000hours.org/podcast/episodes/stuart-russell-human-compatible-ai/

111 'In a 2018 global survey of EAs, AI was ranked the second most important cause area after global poverty': 'EA Survey 2019 Series: Cause Prioritization', Effective Altruism forum, 3 Jan. 2020. forum.effectivealtruism.org/posts/8hExrLibTEgyzaDxW/ea-survey-2019-series-cause-prioritization#Top_causes

113 'The philosopher Kwame Anthony Appiah has a question for the effective altruists': Kwame Anthony Appiah, *Cosmopolitanism: Ethics in a World Full of Strangers* (W.W. Norton, 2006), 158–162.

115 'The 80,000 Hours website lists the two most neglected and important problems in the world as AI risk and pandemic risk reduction": Gregory Lewis, 'Reducing Global Catastrophic Biological Risks', 80,000 Hours, March 2020. 80000hours.org/problem-profiles/global-catastrophic-biological-risks/#what-are-global-catastrophic-biological-risks

— 'In the 2019 EA survey, when asked, "Which cause should be the top priority?", climate change was the second most popular choice, after global poverty': 'EA Survey 2019 Series: Cause Prioritization', Effective Altruism forum, 3 Jan. 2020. forum.effectivealtruism.org/posts/8hExrLibTEgyzaDxW/ea-survey-2019-series-cause-prioritization#Top_causes

118 'a full-fledged qualia economy': 'Wireheading Done Right', *Qualia Computing*, 20 Aug. 2016. qualiacomputing.com/2016/08/20/wireheading_done_right/

119 'The main value (or disvalue) of intelligence would be to explore physics further': Brian Tomasik, 'Is There Suffering in Fundamental Physics?', *Reducing Suffering* (blog), 17 Aug. 2014. reducing-suffering.org/is-there-suffering-in-fundamental-physics/

121 'One of Singer's most controversial ideas is that of "the expanding moral circle"': Peter Singer, *The Expanding Circle: Ethics, Evolution, and Moral Progress* (Princeton University Press, 2011; first published 1981).

— 'Effective altruism, so far at least, has been a conservative movement': Amia Srinivasan, 'Stop the Robot Apocalypse', *London Review of Books* 37, no. 18 (24 Sept. 2015). lrb.co.uk/the-paper/v37/n18/amia-srinivasan/stop-the-robot-apocalypse

126 'Indeed, at hearing the news that "the old god is dead", we philosophers and "free spirits" feel illuminated by a new dawn': Friedrich Nietzsche, Book 5 of *The Gay Science* (1882), cited in *Reasons and Persons*, ii.

129 'Life can be wonderful as well as terrible': Derek Parfit, *On What Matters*, vol. 2 (Oxford University Press, 2013), 618.

The Hunger and the Rain

130 'Everyone young going down the long slide / To happiness, endlessly': Philip Larkin, 'High Windows', Poetry Foundation. poetryfoundation. org/poems/48417/high-windows (accessed 5 Nov. 2020)

138 'There's a classic study in the obesity and food addition literature': Janet Ng, Eric Stice, Sonja Yokum and Cara Bohon, 'An fMRI Study of Obesity, Food Reward, and Perceived Caloric Density. Does a Low-Fat Label Make Food Less Appealing?', *Appetite* 57, no. 1 (Aug. 2011): 65–72. doi.org/10.1016/j.appet.2011.03.017

149 'We are survival machines, robot vehicles blindly programmed': Richard Dawkins, *The Selfish Gene* (30th anniversary edition, Oxford University Press, 2006), xxi.

151 'In one of his later books, Dawkins shows how the evolutionary process explores genetic space': The book to which I am referring is *The Extended Phenotype* (Oxford University Press, 1982).

170 'The world shines in the radiance of advances, advantages and material goods': Heidegger, *Collected Edition*, vol. 77 (Vittorio Klostermann, 1976), 216.

174 'Hannah Arendt called him "the secret king of thought"': George Steiner, 'The Magician in Love', *Times Literary Supplement*, 1999. the-tls.co.uk/articles/george-steiner-briefe-1925-1975-hannah-arendt-martin-heidegger-book-review/

175 *Being and Time*, Heidegger's most famous work, was first published in 1927. Its first English translation was published in 1962.

176 'In 1966 Heidegger agreed to an interview with *Der Spiegel*': A full English translation can be read at the Internet Archive, archive.org/details/MartinHeidegger-DerSpiegelInterviewenglishTranslationonly AGodCan (accessed 27 Oct. 2020)